MEXICAN AMERICAN BASEBALL IN THE ALAMO REGION

They Played Their Way; With Love, Con Corazon

His cap flew off as he went flying around the bases . . .
A hot ground-hugging grounder . . . glove down on the ground,
eyes on the ball, "Smooth Hands" Sandy Sandoval fields it smoothly,
flips it to "Sure Hands" Hidalgo who whips it over to "Money" Montoya
at first to complete a game-ending double play. (Only a handful
in the big leagues turn the double play with such skill.)

Rounding third base forcing an errant throw . . .
It wasn't the home runs that got him a shot at the next level
or the towering blast he proudly dedicated to his parents
who'd immigrated from Mexico long ago. It wasn't
the big league scout coming up to him after a game
to shake his hand with a firm signing offer before the service years.
Racing from second base to make an over the shoulder catch
in shallow right field . . . It wasn't the huge crowds
from other barrios that came to see him play.

It was the look in Guadalupe's eyes that inspired and motivated him
that he most cherished. The look in her eyes reflecting his love for her
through the thin years, the war, the children, family responsibilities,
her night classes and career as a pediatric nurse, his solid 12 years
in the majors and career as an international scout. Now and then
the photo album the grandchildren love to dwell over comes out.
Now and then a story, un recuerdo, Sandy affectionately shares
with his Lupita, his inspiration, his corazon.

Ron Baca
September 23, 2014

Ron Baca is a retired Los Angeles public school special-education teacher and a poet/activist. His fifth chapbook, *An Everlasting Song*, was published in March 2015. He is a frequent reader at Avenue 50 Studio in Highland Park. The title of this poem is from a line in Tomas Benitez's poem "They Played This Game, Baseball."

FRONT COVER:
Richard C. Zamora takes a cut for the camera. He played for the Moonglow Athletic Club, which was part of the Hot Wells League on the Southside of San Antonio in the 1950s. (Courtesy of Richard C. Zamora.)

COVER BACKGROUND:
The Bluebirds were based in San Ygnacio, in Zapata County, Texas. The team played challengers mostly in the southern parts of the state during the 1930s. By 1942, the club broke up, as most of the members joined the armed forces to serve in World War II. (Courtesy of Dr. Cruz C. Torres.)

BACK COVER:
As Pedro Méndez got better and his skills began to shine on the diamond, the old guys took notice. This team, with longtime friend and Spanish American player Rudy Guerrero—who himself had passed his prime—was chock full of old-timers. (Courtesy of Pedro Méndez.)

MEXICAN AMERICAN BASEBALL IN THE ALAMO REGION

Richard A. Santillán, Jorge Iber, Grace G. Charles,
Alberto Rodríguez, and Gregory Garrett
Foreword by Arnoldo De León

ARCADIA
PUBLISHING

Published by Arcadia Publishing
Charleston, South Carolina

Library of Congress Control Number: 2014958532

For all general information, please contact Arcadia Publishing:
Telephone 843-853-2070
Fax 843-853-0044
E-mail sales@arcadiapublishing.com
For customer service and orders:
Toll-Free 1-888-313-2665

Visit us on the Internet at www.arcadiapublishing.com

Para mis padres, Carlos Veloz and Rachel Oviedo Santillán, mis hermanos y sus esposas, Charles and Sandy, Joe and Eva, and to my wife, Teresa, who has been the perfect game of my life.

—Richard

To my father, Joe M. Guajardo, who loved music and baseball and instilled in me an appreciation of them.

—Grace

To my wife, Raquel, and our son Matthew, you two make everything worthwhile. And to my father, Manuel, the person who is most responsible for getting me hooked on the wonderful game of baseball, and for the wonderful memories of Sunday morning softball games all over Little Havana in the 1970s.

—Jorge

To Rene Torres, for his wonderful work on Mexican/Mexican Americans in sports in the Lower Rio Grande Valley and Northern Mexico. Also to Janette García and her wonderful staff at the Lower Rio Grand Valley Special Collections at the University of Texas–Pan American, and to my history department at Texas A&M University at Kingsville.

—Alberto

For my father, Monty Joe Garrett, the man who bought me my first glove. I hope you're proud of your "little boy," dad.

—Gregory

CONTENTS

ACKNOWLEDGMENTS

The foundation of this project to publicize the rich history of Mexican American baseball and softball in the Texas Alamo region is due to the remarkable work of the Latino Baseball History Project at California State University, San Bernardino (CSUSB). Planning committee members for the project include Dean Cesar Caballero, Iwona Contreras, Richard A. Santillán, Terry A. Cannon, Tomas Benitez, Mark A. Ocegueda, Cherstin Lyon, Jill Vassilakos-Long (head of archives and special collections), and Manny Veron. Others who have contributed to this book are Ericka Saucedo, Amina Romero, and Alyssa Rosales.

The authors are indebted to the players and their families who provided treasures of photographs and extraordinary oral histories. These dedicated individuals and groups include Gene Chávez, Jody L. and Gabriel A. López, Roy Álvarez, Carlos Salazar, Joe Livernois, John Fernández, John Cardona, Louis Valverde, Phyllis Pérez, Randy Zaragoza, Richard Soto, Al Moreno, Bea Dever, Audrey F. Garza, Rio Grande Valley Sports Hall of Fame, the Southwest Collection Archives at Texas Tech University, the *Laredo Times*, Lupita Barrera, Lynn Yakubik, Kimberly Kelly, Priscilla, Curtis and Stan Garrett, the Zamoras (Richard, Tony, Robert, and Raul), Joe Sánchez, Donald Falcón, Mario Longoria, Val Estrello, Charlie Calderon, the New Braunfels West End Lions, Estella and Bobby Farias, Frank Chapa, Pedro Méndez, David Rutherford, Tomas Molina Jr., Eliseo Cadenas, Lisa Neely, Lolo Treviño, the Institute of Texan Cultures in San Antonio, and the Ethnic and Women's Studies Department and the Cesar E. Chávez Center at California State University at Pomona.

A special thanks to all of the authors, whose tireless work and incredible energy made this book possible. We recognize again the professional work and patience of our in-house editor, Elisa Grajeda-Urmston, and offer distinct appreciation to our technical consultant, Monse Segura. Last, but not least, our heartfelt respect goes to Arcadia Publishing and our remarkable editors Michael G. Kinsella and Jeff Ruetsche.

All images in chapter four are courtesy of the Lower Rio Grande Valley Collection at the University of Texas–Pan American.

Unless otherwise noted, all images are courtesy of the Latino Baseball History Project.

FOREWORD

I first witnessed baseball as part of Mexican American community life while growing up in rural Texas at a place named Chapman Ranch. There, my father, Jesús De León, played for a team called the Chapman Ranch Steers. Their field was in the midst of a pasture, part of it cleared away for games. The team was comprised of farmhands—they all worked the cotton fields through the week and relieved the stress of hard labor (and poverty) by taking to the diamond on summer Sundays. Each player provided his own glove and spikes; the manager purchased the uniforms, bats, and balls.

The ambience was overwhelmingly Mexican, with Spanish-surname competitors usually driving in from nearby Corpus Christi. From behind the backstop or from the hoods of cars, family members yelled lustily (in Spanish, of course), encouraging fathers and brothers. Would-be entrepreneurs brought taquitos or sundry eats to sell. Umpires made calls in English, but we interpreted the language as being Spanish.

I had no historical consciousness then. I saw the games as just another amusement. Deep into my scholarly career, I considered baseball outings as being but a pastime. In some of my early works, I did refer to baseball, but I treated it cursorily and categorized it as mere "leisure activity." Recent essays on Tejano sports, however, have persuaded me that the baseball field is equal in importance to such subjects as community building, labor, immigration, and politics, among others. These recent pioneering works suggest that much more remains to be explored. Yet to be told, for instance, are the achievements of individuals and teams at the high school, college, and professional levels. Because of Texas's regional diversity, historians might wish to compare the different manner by which rural communities, such as Fort Stockton in West Texas, and urban areas, like Houston, went about organizing, scheduling, and playing the game, for example.

This volume is certain to stimulate interest in such topics. Texas is rich in Mexican history—much still untold. We are happy that the Latino Baseball History Project has given Tejano baseball the space it deserves.

—Arnoldo De León
C.J. "Red" Davidson Professor of History
Angelo State University

INTRODUCTION

The study of Mexican Americans in Texas has been a focus of scholars and popular writers for more than 80 years. These authors, both within and outside of academia, have examined a multitude of aspects of this extraordinary story, including community building, labor organizing, politics, religion, immigration, education, and the role of women. One area that has not garnered sufficient research has been the role of sports, particularly baseball, as part of individual and communal lives of Spanish-surname persons in the state (though that is changing). Using the community-based empowerment model that Dr. Richard A. Santillán developed for baseball and softball in California, this book offers a first survey of this topic in the Lone Star State.

Within these pages, readers will find breathtaking photographs and amazing recollections of men and women who played the sport throughout Texas, with emphasis on the corridor from San Antonio to Corpus Christi. While it is easy to assume that ball games, especially those on Sundays, served merely a recreational purpose, there was much more to such social gatherings. The photos contained herein testify to baseball's power as a mechanism with which to hold to, and celebrate, cultural identify in the face of great racial difficulties. Success on the diamond was used to challenge stereotypes about the physical and intellectual capabilities of Mexicanos that were all too prevalent among the majority population in years past. For example, the 1949 El Paso Bowie High School team won the state title in baseball while overcoming mistreatment throughout the state because its players were of Mexican descent.

In other words, success in baseball, whether in community, scholastic, semipro, or professional leagues, was a valuable tool to show that Spanish speakers could compete effectively in a sport that most Texans valued. If they were able to accomplish impressive feats in baseball, and later softball, what else were "they" capable of? The pages that follow provide but a glimpse of the extensive photographic and anecdotal evidence of how significant baseball was, and is, to Mexican American life in Texas.

—Jorge Iber, PhD
Texas Tech University

1

SAN ANTONIO

There are ghosts in this city. Ghosts of San Antonio's past are quickly brought up in conversations among those who remember them: Leal Street Diamond; Escobar Field, named after Eleterio; Burrows Field at Old South San High School; Van Daele Stadium, across the street from Old Mission Stadium; Pittman Sullivan; the Polo Field at Brackenridge Park; Richter Field at Laredo and Santa Rosa; De la Garza Field; and even Sánchez Spencer Field. The *peloteros* recall the memories fondly. These were the fields they aspired to play on as each generation grew up watching the last. From the Catholic Youth Organization, to high school ball, to unorganized semipro leagues, to the Spanish American League—each decade creating new memories. On these fields, a man was not defined by the color of his skin or what side of town he was from. He was defined by his ability to throw a ball, swing a bat, and field with a glove. The ghosts will always be in this city.

Few Texans are unaware of the influence Mexico has had on the city of San Antonio, evident in the architecture, music, and endless culinary delights. All of these have helped to establish a strong Mexican American culture that is a timeless presence on the banks of the San Antonio River. What many do not realize, or just have not thought about in years, is the role of baseball in defining the identity of this tight-knit community. When players begin to talk about Sundays at the fields named above, their eyes light up and smiles emerge. They remember the grandstands full of families and children. They remember the competitive spirit it engendered among the teams, and the lasting friendships this competition forged. They remember mariachi bands, restaurants, and cantinas. All of these come together to solidify a community and reaffirm the importance of the game to the men who played it and the community that rooted for them.

The Stonewall Grocery team, posing here in 1953, was one of the better teams that played around San Antonio that year. The majority of these players were in their early twenties. Stonewall Grocery played at Van Daele Stadium in San Antonio, one of the many neighborhood stadiums no longer around. Richard C. Zamora, Gilbert Bailey, Rudy Gonzáles, the Villanueva brothers Bobby and Richard, George Rodríguez, and Louie Martínez, all lifelong friends, were part of this team. (Courtesy of Richard C. Zamora.)

Richard C. Zamora, of the Moonglow Athletic Club baseball team, is seen here around 1952. The Moonglow club was a member of the Hot Wells League, which played on the south side of San Antonio. This picture was taken at Burrows Field in South San. The outfield was unfenced from center field all the way to the foul line in right field. In fact, deep right field was used as the parking lot on game days. All of the Zamora brothers played on Burrows Field at one time or another. (Courtesy of Richard C. Zamora.)

The Texans were sponsored by Hippo Size, an old San Antonio soda water distributor. The baseball club is seen here at a game in Houston. The Hippo Size Soda Company was run by Silverio Garza of San Antonio. Oftentimes, local business owners would sponsor these teams as both a moneymaker for San Antonio crowds and as a means of getting a bit of free advertising. The Mexican American business community played a major part in financing many local semipro teams. Among those shown here are (first row) Jerry Vaca (far left), Kino Espinoza (fifth from left), and Gilbert Bailey (far right); (second row) Armando Villareal (second from left), Henry García (fifth from left), Amado Frias (sixth from left), Herbert Alonzo (third from right), ? Rodríguez (second from right), Richard C. Zamora (far right). (Courtesy of Richard C. Zamora.)

The Central Catholic High School of San Antonio baseball team poses around 1986. Coach Richard C. Zamora had another solid team on his hands this year. Zamora was able to coach through the 1990 season with Central Catholic. He gave 40 years to the baseball community as a player and coach. It allowed him an opportunity to influence a lot of young men in the South San community. He taught them baseball as well as principles that would help them later in life. In an interview, Coach Zamora recalled several "teaching" moments, some serious, and others comical. (Courtesy of Richard C. Zamora.)

St. John's Berchman was a San Antonio Catholic Youth Organization team. Teams like this allowed Richard C. Zamora (right rear) to give back some of his knowledge of the diamond to the community. On this team in the early 1970s, he coached his son, Michael Zamora (first row, far right). Assistant coach Arturo Domínguez (left rear) helped Coach Zamora with the team. Catholic Youth Organization was an important part of youth baseball in South San Antonio, giving many kids an opportunity at team sports and all they offer. (Courtesy of Richard C. Zamora.)

14th Annual
Latin American State
Softball Tournament
AUGUST 10 and 11, 1963
MEMORIAL PARK   HOUSTON, TEXAS
Championship Game Sunday 8:30 P.M.

HIPPO of San Antonio
LATIN-AMERICAN STATE CHAMPIONS, 1960, 61, 62
RUSK A.C. TOURNAMENT COMMITTEE

This is the program cover for the 14th annual Latin American State Softball Tournament in Houston. Fast-pitch softball teams from the Latin and Mexican American communities would travel there from around the state. The Hippo Size Soda teams from San Antonio were a powerhouse, winning the championship in 1960, 1961, and 1962. These tournaments were always very competitive and showcased some of the elite fast-pitch talent in the state of Texas. (Courtesy of Richard C. Zamora.)

Pictured here is the Royal Palace Baseball Club in the late 1970s. Many of the college and semipro teams featured the same groups of players. (Courtesy of Richard C. Zamora.)

This is one of the many fast-pitch softball teams that participated in league play around San Antonio. It consisted of several individuals who played with each other at St. Mary's University in San Antonio. The teammates and their connection to each other did not end with their college experience. Lifetime connections were made on the diamond, whether the bases were 60 or 90 feet apart. Michael Zamora is in the center with arms crossed. His father also played fast-pitch in leagues around San Antonio in the 1960s and 1970s. (Courtesy of Richard C. Zamora.)

This is a pitcher for the Royal Palace semipro team. Royal Palace was a locally owned business in South San. Several teams offered young Mexican Americans the opportunity to play and even make a buck or two. This team comprised several members who also played with St. Mary's University in San Antonio. Players would use teams like the Royal Palace club to keep themselves in shape for the St. Mary's season. It is believed that this player is standing in front of the St. Mary's team bus. (Courtesy of Richard C. Zamora.)

Fast-pitch softball was competitive, but it also offered a chance at fellowship, as seen with this team sponsored by Pabst Blue Ribbon. The team consisted of old friends who had been together for a while on both the baseball and softball diamond. Richard C. Zamora, Rudy Gonzáles, and Arturo Hernandez had played on several teams together, both hardball and softball. Relationships built on the diamond created lifelong friends among individuals in the communities of South San. (Courtesy of Richard C. Zamora.)

San Antonio saw extensive Little League participation by Mexican American communities. This is the Little Flower team, part of the Little Flower Basilica organization. The players are, from left to right, (first row) unidentified, Charlie Calderon, Danny Morales, Ernie Zatterein, Freddy Morales, Val Estrello, and Héctor Molina; (second row) Henry Vara, unidentified, Danny Flores, Donald Falcón, Noey Lozano, and unidentified. (Courtesy of Charlie Calderon.)

Winding down after the game was common. This is one of Richard C. Zamora's teams at the Lone Star Brewery in San Antonio. Lone Star was an active sponsor in several leagues around San Antonio, no doubt to the delight of many of the players. (Courtesy of Richard C. Zamora.)

Friendships were made that lasted for lifetimes, as shown here. Many of these men played ball together at some point while growing up in San Antonio. This softball team was simply an extension of those friendships forged on the diamond. (Courtesy of Richard C. Zamora.)

This Little Flowers team has brought in a ringer from the Ernie's Place squad. This is an example of a local business sponsoring an individual uniform. Charlie Calderon admits that sponsors would sometimes place their logos on the front of a uniform and move the company name to the back. The sponsors saw it as a great opportunity to advertise to the parents. Among Calderon's buddies in this photograph are Donald Falcón, Henry Vara, and Danny Morales. (Courtesy of Charlie Calderon.)

The Varsity ball club won the Spanish American League in 1968, defeating the Garza Finance team in the championship game. Donald Falcón, Leroy Ihrer, and Danny Galindo hit solo home runs for Varsity. Competition among the Spanish American teams was fierce, but many of the players became lifelong friends because of their participation in the league. Raul Martínez and Val Estrello also played on this 1968 varsity club. (Courtesy of Donald Falcón.)

The San Antonio Edgewood High School baseball team poses for a photograph in 1965. The team won the Texas 4-A championship that year. (Courtesy of Donald Falcón.)

This is the Kelly Air Force Base Civilians fast-pitch softball team, comprising employees at Kelly AFB in San Antonio. This team was always competitive against the squads that played for base championships. Gilbert Bailey, Richard C. Zamora, Anthony Gonzáles, Rudy Gonzáles, and Martin Rodríguez had played with each other on several San Antonio hardball and softball teams. (Courtesy of Richard C. Zamora.)

The San Antonio Jefferson High School team was able to pull off a state championship run. The squad was coached by Raul Zamora (standing, far right), who had done his part to help South San High School to a state title himself. He played ball at Baylor University in Waco before returning to San Antonio and becoming active in the South San community, as did the entire Zamora family. (Courtesy of Richard C. Zamora.)

Pictured here are Sandy Sánchez (left) and Dan Salinas. These men carried themselves well in the Spanish American League of San Antonio, where they enjoyed long careers. Each was quick to mentor younger guys and create a sense of solidarity among their teammates. (Courtesy of Joe Sánchez.)

Sandy Sánchez poses in full catcher's regalia. He was one of the stronger backstops in the Spanish American League. This photograph is important, as it offers a glimpse of one of the Span-Am ghosts, Polo Field at Brackenridge Park. Numerous games were held here from 1946 to 1953. Like many of the stadiums of the Span-Am league, it was packed with families and community members every Sunday. All enjoyed high-quality baseball in an environment that allowed them a respite from the adversities of the outside world. (Courtesy of Joe Sánchez.)

This is a beautiful image of the 1957 Saldaña Food Stores ball club of the Spanish American League in San Antonio. The photograph was taken within the confines of Richter Field, with Old Mission Stadium in the background. These two fields were hubs for the baseball community in San Antonio. This squad won both the city and state championships that year. Shown are, from left to right, (first row) Joe Sánchez, Bruno Villareal, Jim Knieski, Sandy Sánchez, Joe Rodríguez, Rene Urbanowich, and Ralph Sánchez; (second row) Gilbert Delgado, Joe Calderon, Robert Chapa, unidentified, Bobby Owens, Pete Correa, and Freddie Sánchez; (third row) Charley Montemayor, Gilbert Díaz, Jimmy Allison, Albert López, Alex DeLa Garza, Bubba Wagner, and Joe Harlen. (Courtesy of Joe Sánchez.)

Saldaña Food Stores was a powerhouse in the Spanish American League. This is the Saldaña club at Richter Field in 1954, the year that the Spanish American League began playing at this field. For a while, this location, with Old Mission Stadium next door, was the baseball pulse of the community and even the city. Posing are, from left to right, (first row) Bobby Pacheco, two unidentified, Jim Knieski, Fred Sánchez Jr. (son of Sandy), Roger Tash, Johnny Gutiérrez, Raj Arocha, and unidentified; (second row) Alfred Sánchez, Steve López, Noah Rodríguez, unidentified, Gilbert Díaz, Ed Quissenberry, Joe Naranjo, Roy Vargas, and Buddy Lozano. (Courtesy of Joe Sánchez.)

The Garza Finance Co. ball club won both the Spanish American League and the city championship in 1965–1966. This team was definitely a family affair, with players Sandy and Joe Sánchez and bat girl Patricia Sánchez. From left to right are (first row) bat boy Raymond Leyva and bat girl Patricia Sánchez; (second row) Louis Davila, Garnet Steubing, Ben Jonietz, Ken Floyd, Bill Green, and Genero Krausse; (third row) John Villanueva, Jim Burkett, Billy Dunam, Fidel Álvarado, Jay McCarty, and Earl Taborn; (fourth row) coach Pat Sigma, Chon Garza, Sandy Sánchez, Ron Mercer, Gene Culpepper, Joe Sánchez, John Rodríguez, and Ernie Martínez.

The 1950 Fred's Place team won the Spanish American League championship. Fred's Place was an excellent Mexican restaurant, owned by Fred Rodríguez. Shown are, from left to right, (first row) Ralph and Joe Sánchez, sons of manager Sandy Sánchez; (second row) Fred Rodríguez, Bernard Reyes, Luther Chapa, Marty Rodríguez, Gilbert Delgado, Noah Rodríguez, and Rudy Guerrero; (third row) Willie Doria, Joe Rodríguez, Tony Traveaso, Bobby Chapa, Bruno Villareal, and manager Alfred Sánchez. (Courtesy of Joe Sánchez.)

This is the 1952 Grand Prize Beer team of the Spanish American League. Several breweries and distributors, like Lone Star and Pabst Blue Ribbon, sponsored teams throughout San Antonio. Posing are, from left to right, (first row) Ralph Sánchez, Freddie Sánchez, and Eddie Arevalos; (second row) unidentified, Joe Morín, Bruno Villareal, Joe Rodríguez, Ernest Arceniega, Tom Arevalos Sr., and Luther Chapa; (third row) Fred Moya, Jim Sweeney, Joe Calderon Jr., Tony Delfin, Willie Doria, Marty Rodríguez, Bobby Owens, Robert Chapa, R.G. Méndez, and Sandy Sánchez. (Courtesy of Joe Sánchez.)

This shot catches a glimpse of everyday life in the barrios of San Antonio. A crew like this was regularly seen on a Sunday afternoon, according to Donald Falcón. Falcón's father, Emmanuel Marshall Falcón, is pictured kneeling in the center with his cap bill turned up. They were usually headed to the closest empty lot with bats, gloves, and balls in tow. They built lasting friendships all because of the diamond. (Courtesy of Donald Falcón.)

This is the Cardona team of the Spanish American League in San Antonio. Like most of the Spanish American teams, these players suited up with pride. Note the crisp white uniforms. Care was taken to stack the bats and lay the catcher's gear out just right. These guys were serious about their craft, and it showed in the way they carried themselves. They were part of *los peloteros*, a brotherhood. To these players, who were once kids playing in the empty lots of San Antonio, they had made it to the show. (Courtesy of Joe Sánchez.)

These are the 1926 Aztecs, the champs of the West Side of San Antonio. The Aztecs played other semipro teams of the time, and the competition around town was fierce. The Aztecs organized and began playing early on, in 1926, predating the Spanish American League. Pictured are, clockwise from top left, C. Pérez, I. Gans, Earl Meyer, T. Salas, P. Monsalro, P. Garza, J. Vargas, D. Garza, M. Villareal, H. Satcher, J. Bernal, P. Sánchez, and J. Rendón. (Courtesy of University of Texas–San Antonio Special Collections.)

Shown here are three players of the San Antonio Missions minor league team. The "Missions" name has been used in some form or other since the creation of a team as a charter member of the Texas League in 1888. The player at center is Precoppio Herrera, one of the more renowned Mexican American players the Missions had. An excellent ballplayer, he was a man around town and known as quite the character. Note that he is posing for this newspaper photograph *sin pantalones*! (Courtesy of University of Texas–San Antonio Special Collections.)

2

CORPUS CHRISTI

In 1810, the Corpus Christi region was known as Rincón Del Oso (the corner of the bear), and grazing cattle was a profitable enterprise. In the 1850 census, Mexicans were living along the coast in one-room *jacales*. They were farmers, sheepherders, and fisherman. They brought cartloads of oyster shells to build roads and sometimes served as policemen and lamplighters. In order to understand the emergence of baseball in Corpus Christi, this chapter devotes several introductory photos to the historical social, cultural, economical, and political leadership that existed many years ago.

Mexicans brought with them their traditions, culture, and language. These men and women of vision were builders, settling in a new land. La Colonia Mexicana had its own festivities, parades, bands, and social activities. By the turn of the 20th century, Vicente Lozano had his own merchandise dry-goods store. T.B. Rivera owned a store, and Rafael Galván built his business along the shore. Lozano and Galván were just a few to own property and build homes. Men and women formed mutual-aid organizations to help the poor and the sick with funds collected within these associations. Both brave men and women stood together to raise their voices for equal rights as citizens of the United States. In 1929, three large organizations came together to form the largest and longest-lasting such group in the United States, the League of United Latin American Citizens, led by Ben Garza.

In 1897, some of the men formed their own baseball team, playing in Mexico. Later, young girls and boys formed their own social clubs, and young boys and men played baseball for entertainment. World War II came, and most of these young men left for the war. Some never returned, and others came home to find the same discrimination, tuberculosis, segregation, and unemployment. Fighting for this country's freedom did not earn them appreciation or equal rights. They were still unwanted Mexicans returning from yet another war to pick cotton and dig ditches. Among those returning was Capt. Dr. Héctor P. García, later founder of the American G.I. Forum. García returned to live in Corpus Christi. His office was situated on the west side of town. He helped the poor and aided veterans in their fight against racism and bigotry. Presidents and politicians courted him for the Mexican American vote. Dr. García was awarded the country's highest award, the Medal of Freedom.

Members of the Mexican American Women's Auxiliary, part of the Woodmen of the World organization, gather at Obreros Hall. Among those pictured are Virginia Reyes Galván, Ventura Zamudio Sánchez, Mrs. Microvich, and Joséfa Téllez. These women worked to raise funds to help the sick and the poor of the community. (Courtesy of the Rafael and Virginia Galván Collection.)

Sociedad Concordia was formed to help the Mexican community. Due to the large number of Mexicans living in the area, several organizations were founded, each obliged to help the poor with medical bills, funeral expenses, and food and clothing. Those identified here are Joséfa Téllez (seated, far left) and Virginia Reyes Galván (seated, far right), wife of Rafael Galván, baseball player and owner of local businesses. (Courtesy of Rafael Galván Sr. and Virginia Galván Collection.)

Seen here are members of the Sons of America, Local Council No. 4, in 1929. This patriotic group poses in front of the Methodist Church in Corpus Christi. They later became one of the three large organizations to unite as the League of United Latin American Citizens. In the first row, holding the flag, is Ben Garza. He became the first president of the league, which became one of the largest and longest-lasting organizations to represent Latin Americans. (Courtesy of the Rafael and Virginia Galván Collection.)

The Orden Mutual de Obreros y Obreras was founded in 1916. Here, *obreros* march on east Lipan Street in a parade marking the 14th anniversary of the organization. Conrad Rodríguez formed the guard and band. The organization had 900 members who paid dues and raised funds to help the people in La Colonia Mexicana. (Courtesy of Richard R. Fuentes and Joséfina B. Fuentes family Papers.)

Obreras dressed in similar outfits representing their organization march in the parade on Lipan Street in 1930. They had to represent the organization with integrity, raise funds, engage in activities, and be faithful in their attendance and dues. (Courtesy of Richard R. Fuentes and Joséfine B. Fuentes family Papers.)

This building is the Orden Fraternidad de Obreros y Obreras Hall. It held various business meetings, dances, and festivities of the Mexican community. The hall became famous—it was here that the League of United Latin American Citizens was formed in 1929. (Courtesy of Richard R. Fuentes and Joséfine B. Fuentes family Papers.)

The Woodmen of the World Camp No. 2126 is represented in the parade. The decorated car was followed by men dressed in uniforms. The parade took place in Corpus Christi in 1930. (Courtesy of Richard R. Fuentes and Joséfine B. Fuentes family Papers.)

Women dressed in costumes representing W.C. Grove 722 ride in a decorated car. The Mexican community held its own parades and celebrations on the streets of Corpus Christi. Their customs and flags represented their mother country of Mexico. (Courtesy of Richard R. Fuentes and Joséfine B. Fuentes family Papers.)

This photograph depicts José A. Gallardo's Real Jazz Orchestra. Gallardo was born in Guanajuato, Mexico, and raised in Corpus Christi. His father taught him how to play the violin at an early age. Later, he became a pianist and moved to Laredo, where he started his own jazz group, the Syncopaters. Gallardo and his orchestra moved to Corpus Christi, playing at dances during the holidays, and at weddings, birthdays, and festivals throughout South Texas. When he retired, he taught piano at his home to youngsters, charging only $5 a month for lessons. (Courtesy of José and Virginia Gallardo Papers.)

The Hi-Fairness Girls Club poses in 1940. In the 1920s, Mexican girls and boys began to form their own social clubs. This was their way of socializing, as they were not comfortable at activities with white students. At the time, few Mexican American girls and boys attended school. In 1929, a group of girls found that they had fun being together, so they formed their own social club. They held dances, picnics, and parties, and raised funds and became involved in the community. (Courtesy of Ryna Donnor Papers.)

The Scorpion Boys Club poses sometime between 1938 and 1940. Mexican boys in the area started forming their own clubs, holding dances, sporting events, and social activities. The first members, seen here, are Onfre Abraca, Carlos García, Ernest Falcón, Frank Platez, Adolph Falcón, John Pérez, Ray García, Ralph Tamez, Frank Leones, John Presas, Ernest Barrera, Lico Liaco, Abel Cortéz, and Henry Trujillo. Presas was killed in World War II. (Courtesy of Ryna Donnor Papers.)

Vicente Lozano (third from left) was one of the early pioneers to arrive in Corpus Christi in the late 1800s. He was a merchant and businessman. White candidates would come to ask him for his opinion on matters pertaining to the city. He was the first Mexican to serve on a criminal district court jury, in 1931. He played baseball with the Los Flacos team. He owned the Southern Select Beer Company, which sponsored a baseball team. His son Gabe became the first Mexican American mayor of Corpus Christi.

Rafael Galván, a Corpus Christi pioneer, arrived in the late 1800s. A man of vision and ideas, he counted among his friends Lyndon B. Johnson, Lázaro Cárdenas (president of Mexico), Rafael Méndez (trumpet player), Richard Kleberg (of the King Ranch), Robert Driscoll (civic leader), and Roy Miller (mayor). His four sons had their own orchestras. Galván played with the Las Águilas and the Los Gordos baseball teams in the 1920s. (Courtesy of Galván family Papers.)

Mexicans were the most commonly hired persons to do the work of picking and harvesting cotton. Mexican workers were preferred, as they could be paid lower wages compared to white laborers. They arrived in truckloads early in the morning to pick hundreds of acres of cotton. Men, women, and children performed the stooped labor in the scorching sun until the end of the day. (Vernon Smylie Papers.)

Maj. Héctor P. García was a physician and surgeon, civil rights leader, humanitarian, and politician. After returning from World War II, he moved to Corpus Christi. In 1948, he founded the American GI Forum, an organization of veterans. It would become one of the strongest organizations helping veterans and the poor. On March 26, 1984, Pres. Ronald Reagan presented him with the highest honor awarded a citizen of this country, the Medal of Freedom. García never stopped working on behalf of his people. In 1953, he sponsored the Jr. GI Forum baseball team. (Courtesy of the Dr. Héctor P. García Papers.)

The Corpus Christi Jr. GI Forum baseball team gathers for a photograph. Shown here are, from left to right, (first row) coach Jesse Rivera, Carlos González, Manuel Hassette, Adolfo Espinoza, Dan Bocanegra, Roger Morales, and Ernest Hernández; (second row) Ramón Salinas, Reynaldo Romero, Juan Castillo, Herbert Hernández, Arturo Acuna, Juan Prieto, Ralph Sifuentes, Baldemar García, and Elfero Quesada. Morales played softball and went to Texas A&M University. Hernández became president of the American Jr. GI Forum. The Juniors played 17 games, going 15-2. (Courtesy of Julián and Angelita Rodríguez.)

Julián Rodríguez (first row, second from left) coached his own baseball team in the 1940s in Corpus Christi. (Courtesy of Julián and Angelita Rodríguez Papers.)

The Kirtley Drugs team is seen here in 1940. Most of these young men left to go to war to serve their country. (Vernon Smylie Collection.)

The Southern Select Beer team was sponsored by Vicente Lozano's Southern Select Brewing Company in 1940. Lozano had been a ball player in the 1920s on the Los Gordos team. The members shown here are not identified. (Courtesy of Vernon Smylie Papers.)

The Gómez Pharmacy sponsored baseball teams. These young men pose outside the pharmacy on July 19, 1947. From left to right are (first row) Antonio Fuentes Jr., unidentified, Dr. Rodolfo Barrera, Jesse Pompa, unidentified, and Gómez (son of pharmacy owner); (second row) Wilmot, two unidentified, Gómez Sr., and three unidentified. Pompa was an outstanding pitcher. Gómez Sr. was the owner of the pharmacy and the team sponsor. The team clinched the pennant in 1948. (Courtesy of the Richard and Joséfina B. Fuentes Collection.)

John Ysidro Dickinson was born in Laredo, Texas, in 1906. He played ball for most of his 88 years in South Texas and Mexico. When major leaguers barnstormed through the Laredo area in the years before World War II, Dickinson pitched against Jimmie Foxx, Dixie Walker, Mickey Cochrane, and other stars. He even pitched against Dizzy Dean in the 1920s, when Dean was stationed at Fort Sam Houston in San Antonio. This 1952 photograph shows Dickinson when he played outfield for a team in Mexico City at the Deportivo Hacienda field. (Courtesy of John Y. Dickinson III.)

Héctor Salinas started two college baseball programs from scratch and was a highly successful athletic director. He was a standout pitcher who led Corpus Christi Carroll to its first district crown, in 1961. He lettered at Pan America University from 1965 to 1968 and was an All-American in 1967. He then guided the baseball outfit at Texas Southmost College, before moving on to lead diamond groups at Laredo Junior College and Texas A&M–Corpus Christi. (Courtesy of the Rio Grande Valley Sports Hall of Fame.)

Domingo Peña owned a pharmacy and jewelry store that sponsored the 1948 Jewelers baseball team. Peña is seen here sitting at the far end of the table holding a cigar. He was active in the community, especially the GI Forum. He also had his own local television show, which featured new singers. In 1969, Peña and several Mexican musical groups went to Vietnam to entertain the troops. Sitting to the left of Peña is Julián Rodríguez, and behind him is Samuel Treviño. Standing to the right of Peña is Andrés Vásquez. (Courtesy of Julián Rodríguez.)

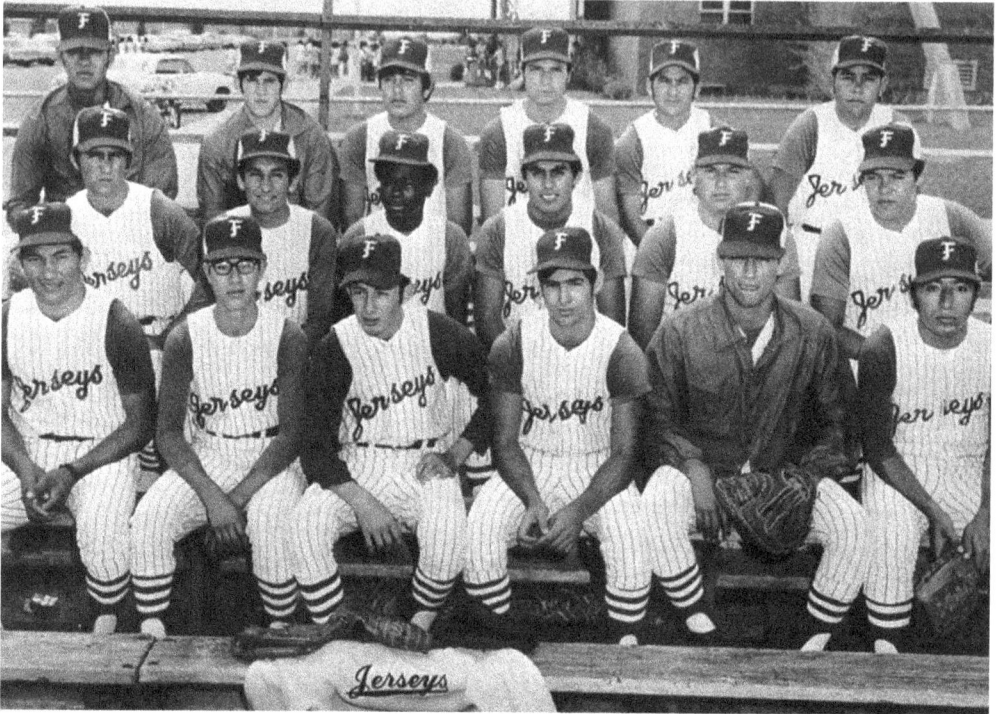

This 1960s Corpus Christi Jerseys team includes, from left to right, (first row) Lisandro Moreno, Ali Garza, Richard Ramírez, John Trad, Johnny Garza, and Carlos Pérez; (second row) Homer Rivera, R.J Méndez, Keith Best, Gonzalo García, David Benavides, and Alfredo García; (third row) Frank Garza, Mario Huerta, Rolando Chavera, Mario Maldonado, and Mario García.

In the 1940s, World War ll veterans returned to a normal way of life. Members of the community passed their spare time watching or playing baseball. The Mexican community's newspapers rallied citizens with news of the city teams. These young men have turned up at Longoria Park on Rabbit Run Road to try out for a team. Among those trying out are Joe Medina Guajardo (No. 4) and his cousin Juan Sánchez (No. 11). They made the R&R Products team during the 1947 season.

This Little League team was sponsored by the Lubbock GI Forum. The American GI Forum raised $300 to buy uniforms for the team. The name of the club was the GI Forum Rockets.

This 1955 Galveston ball team was sponsored during the summer by the Galveston GI Forum. The only person identified is Nieves López, the manager (standing, far right).

This is the LAS League team, which played in the Corpus Christi city league. Andrés Vásquez stands at far left. Julián Rodríguez kneels second from right. Other players are not identified. There were hundreds of young boys and young men who played on countless teams and leagues around the Corpus Christi region. Several teams were sponsored by the Catholic church. One of the best young players during the 1950s was Dan Bocanegra, who lived in the Mexican American community on the west side. At the age of 15, he and his friends played softball and competed against church teams in the city. On Sundays, the team went to church together and then played ball together. Bocanegra's first team with uniforms was the Fire Fighters. In 1954, he played softball with the American Junior GI Forum. He later moved to Whittier, California, in the late 1950s but returned to Corpus Christi in 1974. Bocanegra umpired slow and fast pitch ball and made lots of friends on the softball fields. He later became a scoutmaster, spending time with his sons who were Boy Scouts. He died in 2014.

3

RURAL COUNTIES

The Texas band Asleep at the Wheel sings the words, "I saw miles and miles of Texas." The group's leader, Ray Benson, is definitely onto something. There *are* miles and miles of Texas. Rural life is a matter of fact in the majority of Texas. Upon leaving the urban sprawl of large cities like San Antonio, and even smaller ones like Corpus Christi, a traveler is quickly in the middle of farmland like Medina County, ranchlands like Kleberg County, and hill country like Kendall County. These lands, rural in 2015, were even more isolated in the 1950s. There were far fewer roads in the 1930s. And, four decades before that, roads were merely cart and wagon trails.

Despite this isolation, there is a common thread among all the people in rural Mexican American communities—baseball. These small agricultural towns, where people worked hard during the week, set aside Sundays for church and baseball. The ball fields were pastures, like the one on which the Kowboys played at the King Ranch. Sometimes, an individual would take it upon himself to build a field or, at times, an entire complex, like Felipe Delgado and his work in New Braunfels at West End Park. No matter how unassuming the field, baseball has been played throughout the rural counties of the Alamo region for over a century. Every diamond, regardless of its location, seemed to be filled on Sundays, as the community was there to root for their favorite teams and the athletes who played on them. These Sundays at the ball field helped Mexican Americans cope with some of the harsh realities of everyday life. On the field, players were able to forget these things, and the community was able to cheer with pride. It was often a neighboring town's team that was visiting, and strong rivalries were born. It was also not uncommon for towns along the railroad system to be visited by Mexican national teams, like the Cerveceros, who played for Carta Blanca Beer in Monterrey. These pages reveal some of the faces that made up this group of country ballplayers, who always found time for nine on Sundays, no matter how long the workweek had been.

Mira eres, Las Chismosas! Felipe Delgado and other men in the New Braunfels Mexican American community took to West End Field and competed against each other for bragging rights among the peloteras. These events were often an opportunity for the entire community to be involved and enjoy themselves. On this day, the kids formed lasting memories of *los padres* running around in dresses. Estella Farias, daughter of Felipe Delgado, was quick to point out in her scrapbook, "I can see where some of us got our legs!" (Courtesy of Estella Farias.)

Pictured are Las Chismosas in action. Hopefully, the batter did not hit a double, as there might be problems rounding first. The fans packed this community event at West End Field in New Braunfels, organized by Felipe Delgado. The field's dugouts often flooded after heavy rains. The canvas-covered stands, along with the cantina and restaurant, made for the perfect complex to host the West End Lions, their families, and Las Chismosas. (Courtesy of Estella Farias.)

Felipe Delgado, seen in his straw hat, started his little ball club as the New Braunfels Cardinals in 1947. As is evident here, the guys were obviously good friends. Men like Delgado laid the foundation for groups of young men to play organized ball. This team, later named the New Braunfels West End Lions, played at West End Complex, built and funded by Delgado and community volunteers. (Courtesy of Estella Farias.)

The 1958 New Braunfels West End Lions pose for a team photograph in front of Mr. Bock's local Ford dealership. Sponsoring a successful ball club like the Lions was an excellent way to advertise a business. The team was a symbol of quality, which translated to the cars in the parking lot. The community could take pride in pulling for a class act like the Lions. Shown here are, from left to right, (first row) Lee Alañiz, Joe Mesa, Felipe Delgado, and player/manager/owner Ramón Bustos; (second row) Roberto Cantu, scorekeeper, two unidentified, Randy Biesenbock, Charlie Watney, and Cruz Carillo; (third row) Mr. Bock, Gilbert Campos, unidentified, Leroy "Hook" Pannemill, David Ruterford, unidentified, Bill Strickland, and Raymond Chapa. (Courtesy of Estella Farias.)

Here is the 1953 New Braunfels West End Lions. The team was owned and managed by Felipe Delgado. From left to right are (first row) Jesse Guerrero, Sal Ferrere, unidentified, Pete Campos, and Cruz Carillo; (second row) manager/owner Felipe Delgado, Frank Chapa, Lee Alañiz, Andy Anderson, Dave Rutherford, Joe Guerrero, and Nayo Delgado (Felipe's brother); (third row) Alfredo Pérez, Jessie García, unidentified, Joe Romano, Oscar Cantu, Rogelio Rodríguez, umpire Don Whitney, and scorekeeper Alberto Cantu. (Courtesy of Estella Farias.)

The 1955 New Braunfels West End Lions, a split squad, played at West End Park against such teams as the Stonewall Grocers out of San Antonio. The games were taken very seriously and created community pride when the local Lions beat the out-of-town teams. Posing here are, from left to right, (first row) Rey Sánchez, José Satelo, Jesse Guerrero, unidentified, José Guerrero, and David Moreno; (second row) Beto Cantu, Pedro Méndez, Rubén Guerrero, Felipe Delgado, unidentified, Luke Ortega, unidentified, and Ramón Chapa. (Courtesy of Estella Farias.)

The New Braunfels 1970 F Troop softball team won the New Braunfels Invitational Ladies Softball Tournament after taking down the Swingers 4-2. Not pictured is coach Bobby Farias, who had played for the West End Lions. At least two of the F Troop players had fathers who were involved with the West End Lions baseball team, evidence of how integral the diamond was to the community. Shown here are, from left to right, (first row) Estella Farias, Irma Cruz, unidentified, and Esther Serna; (second row) Esperanza Lagunas, Anna Chapa, Evy Rodríguez, Beatrice Rosales, and Sally Pérez; (third row) Thelma Simmons, Irma Bustos, Melba Barboza, Mary Aguirre, and Marion García. (Courtesy of Estella Farias.)

Kids roller-skate in the dance hall at the West End Lions Complex in New Braunfels. The dance hall was part of a larger complex, which included a restaurant, cantina, and, of course, a baseball field. The complex would fill up every Sunday with families in the grandstands, along with the sound of music and the smell of food. Similar events took place every Sunday in complexes that mirrored the West End. Felipe Delgado was the community activist who got it all started, using his own money and the help of a group of willing volunteers. He built it from the ground up, and it became a place the community was proud of. (Courtesy of Estella Farias.)

Those who wanted to make it on to the West End Lions squad had to establish themselves on the Red Sox. This New Braunfels squad, made up of Lions hopefuls, was sponsored by Our Lady of Perpetual Church. Felipe Delgado kept a close eye on this group; eventually, several of its players joined his Lions team. Posing here are, from left to right, (first row) A. Amaro, F. Amaro, R. Camarano, unidentified, Teo Ríos, and R. Riva; (second row) Jesse Rodríguez, Jesse Sánchez, Frank Chapa, Joe Zavala, Jesse Farris, and Lee Alañiz; (third row) Agapito Campos, Rubén Bustos, Robert Amaro, and Baldemaro Sánchez; (fourth row) Ramón Chapa, Robert Castro, Delio Bustos, Jesse Guerrero, and Mondo Carillo. (Courtesy of Frank Chapa.)

IN LOVING MEMORY

FELIPE DELGADO
August 23, 1920 to June 15, 2002

Pedro Méndez played for baseball and softball squads, both civilian and military, throughout the Southwest. He said that one of the men he most respected from his career on the diamond was Felipe Delgado. Shown here is Delgado's funeral program. All of his players turned out to pay their respects. He had meant so much to the community and to the young men who played for him. Several of them held on to this very program for years. It is amazing that a man could touch so many lives in a community. And to think, he did it using a kid's game—baseball. (Courtesy of Pedro Méndez.)

Pedro Méndez played with the West End Lions and owner Felipe Delgado in New Braunfels. This photograph was taken in the banquet hall of the West End complex that Delgado had put his heart and soul into. In interviews, several of these players said that it was one of the best groups they had played with. Shown here are, from left to right, (first row) Joe Pedadrello, unidentified, Felipe Delgado, Joe Mesa, and Rogelio Rodríguez; (second row) Rubén Guerrero, Pedro Méndez, unidentified, Raymond Chapa, two unidentified, Bill Strickland, and David Moreno; (third row) assistant Beto Cantu, unidentified, Joe Guerrero, unidentified, Delio Gutiérrez, and unidentified. (Courtesy of Pedro Méndez.)

As Pedro Méndez got better and began to shine on the diamond, the old guys took notice. This team was full of old-timers, including longtime friend and Spanish American player Rudy Guerrero, who himself had passed his prime. When Felipe Delgado of the West End Lions approached the young shortstop in 1947, all of his teammates encouraged him to join a team with players on the way up. They knew he would be wasting his talents playing with the old guys. This photograph was taken in 1946 or 1947. Shown here are, from left to right, (first row) unidentified batboy, Aniceto Cortes, three unidentified, Roy Guerrero, Paul Guerrero, and unidentified; (second row) four unidentified, Rudy Guerrero, ? Recendes, Juan Pardo, and manager Frank Gonzáles. (Courtesy of Pedro Méndez.)

San Antonio resident Pedro Méndez played on quite a few squads while growing up in Texas. The one pictured here is the San Marcos Greyhounds. Méndez remembered the team fondly, as it included several of his childhood friends. The players do not seem to have minded that a few spectators joined in. Among those pictured here are Paul Puente, Raymond Méndez, Reynaldo Hernández, Jesse Tennayuca, Paul Contreras, Margarito Pacheco, Joe Contreras, Fidel Guerreo, Celestino Méndez, Raymond Lucio, Robert Turnine, Emilio Contreras, and Pedro Méndez. (Courtesy of Pedro Méndez.)

The San Marcos Blue Sox, seen here in 1955 or 1956, were a solid hardball squad. Pete's brother Raymond played on this team, as did a couple of his cousins. Also on the team was Pete's brother-in-law Armando García. Pete's wife, Alice, had plenty to cheer for at this team's games. It was truly a family affair. The players posing here are, from left to right, (first row) Raúl Ovalle, Johnny Ochoa, Armando García, ? Cisneros, unidentified, and Raymond Lucio; (second row) Raymond Méndez, "Sosa" Sánchez, Bobby Rodríguez, Pedro Méndez, Paul Contreras, and Celestino Méndez. (Courtesy of Pedro Méndez.)

Davis Mountain Air Force Base was home to the 1953 championship fast-pitch softball team the Mustangs, also known as the Hosses. The team qualified for the Air Force Championship Tournament. Before leaving for the tournament, they were able to pick up one player from the other base teams. The player they chose was Pedro Méndez (first row, far right), who was stationed at Davis Mountain. Softball and baseball offered a competitive respite from the grind of military life and a chance to build lasting friendships. Méndez, a resident of San Antonio, is still great friends with the pitcher on this team, Dennis Tasto. He also keeps in touch with Ernie Guerrero. (Courtesy of Pedro Méndez.)

This is the front cover of the program handed out at the Air Force World-Wide Softball tournament. Teams that made it to this tourney had run the gauntlet on their own bases, in their own leagues, and had been crowned champs. It was an opportunity for a huge morale booster for each team's duty station. The Davis Mountain team, the 43rd Bomber Wing, included a young Pedro Méndez. The tournament was held at Amarillo Air Force Base in the Texas Panhandle. The Davis Mountain team did not win that year, but Méndez was proud to have been chosen to be part of the squad. (Courtesy of Pedro Méndez.)

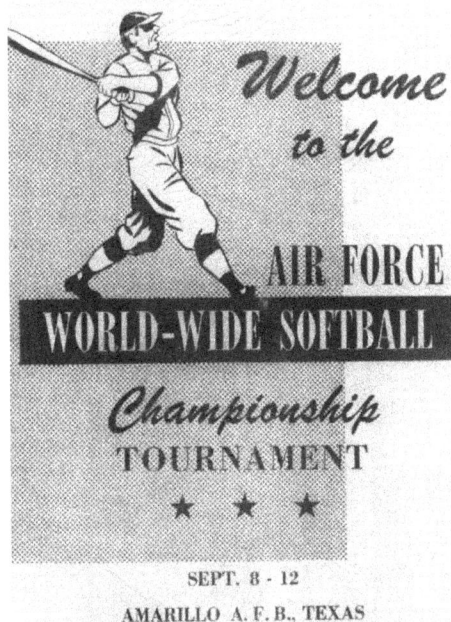

Welcome to the AIR FORCE WORLD-WIDE SOFTBALL Championship TOURNAMENT ★ ★ ★

SEPT. 8 - 12
AMARILLO A. F. B., TEXAS

Pedro Méndez (right) poses here with a couple of his teammates. They all have their hands on the prize. This trophy was awarded at a national hardball tournament. Méndez was one of the starters of the team, but his buddies were no slouches. (Courtesy of Pedro Méndez.)

This unbelievable photograph depicts the 1886 San Diego, Texas, baseball team, Los Únicos. Many of these men became influential members of the San Diego community, and some of them lent their names to the city's streets. Shown are, from left to right, (first row) Avelino García, manager Alfredo Ridder, and Darío G. García; (second row) Loreto García Tovar, Smocker Gravis, Felipe Bodet, Tomas Collins, Arturo D. García, José M. Tovar, and Fidel Pérez. Pérez was reputed to be the "fastest man in Texas" at the time. He is said to have outrun a horse in a competitive footrace. He must have been hell on wheels going from first to third. (Courtesy of Eliseo Cadenas.)

Members of the Alice Mohawk squad from Alice, Texas, in Jim Wells County, pose in 1958 or 1959. The team was coached by Zeke Mora, who is seated at far left. Mora, from Alice, had played in the Texas League in the 1930s and 1940s. Players on the team included Zeke Mora Jr., the coach's boy, and Frankie Domínguez, cousin of the photograph's contributor. Domínguez was the youngest on the squad, but he was solid with a glove and was the team's starting shortstop. (Courtesy of Tomas Molina Jr.)

The Allegros ball club out of San Diego, Texas, stands proud in this photograph. It is a good possibility that this is an all-star team, as players are wearing several different jerseys, including Delta, Red Birds, and Aztecas. San Diego always had several town teams going at any given time. After the season, an all-star team would be assembled that would take on other towns for regional bragging rights. It was a matter of pride to be named to a team like this, and even greater pride to represent the San Diego community. One of the men is believed to be Gilbert Everett Sr., who went on to coach Little League in San Diego in the 1970s. (Courtesy of Tomas Molina Jr.)

The Redbirds of San Diego, Texas, pose around 1935. Included is the contributor's dad, Tomas Molina Sr. (second row, second from left). Adolfo Arguijo (first row, third from left) was very instrumental in the baseball community of San Diego, South Texas, and even Mexico. He spent time there playing for the Cerveceros of the Carta Blanca Brewery in Monterrey. Other players shown here are Luís "el Non" Longoria (first row, second from right) and Domingo "La víbora prieta" Salazar (second row, second from right). These two players also competed in Mexico. (Courtesy of Tomas Molina Jr.)

The Union baseball club of San Diego, Texas, is suited up in the late 19th century. Baseball was a vital part of the community, even in those days. This photograph, one of the oldest in the contributor's collection, dates to around 1890. It was truly a gentleman's game, even in the heat of Texas ranching country. Note the white collared shirts under those "comfortable" wool uniforms. It seems that, on Sundays, the players had only to unclip their ties and throw on their Union tops, strap on shoes, and hit the diamond. (Courtesy of Tomas Molina Jr.)

This is the 500 Club that played baseball at the King Ranch in Kleberg County. (Courtesy of King Ranch Archives.)

The Bruno Rios team of San Diego, Texas, took the field in 1911. These young athletes were the heroes of many, including the grandson of Luis García, Eliseo Cadenas. From left to right are (first row) Telesforo de la Rosa, ? Bustos, and Gaspar Gongora; (second row) Chago Pérez (holding sign), Chito Sendejo, and Luis García; (third row) José M. Aleman, Isabel Navejar, two unidentified, and Antonio Sánchez; (fourth row) Tete Rios (suit and tie), Moises Muñoz, and Juan Treviño (suit and tie). Luis García was the grandfather of the contributor. (Courtesy of Eliseo Cadenas.)

The 1973 Kingsville, Texas, PeeWee League champions show off their trophies. Baldemar Quintanilla coached the team, with help from his son Baldemar Jr. Shown here are, from left to right, (first row) Jerry Ríos, Michael Galindo, Abel Quintanilla, Moises Domínguez, José Vilches, Ricky Salinas, Ernie Pérez, and Max Marroquí; (second row) Jesse Galván, Patrick Albros, Álvaro Flores, Arnulfo Pérez, and Frank Garza; (third row) manager Ward S. Albro; assistant coach Baldemar Quintanilla Jr., and Baldemar Quintanilla Sr. (Courtesy of Ward Albro.)

This is the 1951 King Ranch Cowboys. From left to right are (first row) Jesús García, Alberto Buentello, Romeo Pérez, Alberto Treviño, Billy Buentello, and Alberto Cortéz; (second row) Cesario Cavasos, Jesús Muñoz, Cipriano García, Gilberto Rodríguez, Ramiro Gutiérrez, Jesús Garza, Lorenzo Mendietta, Nerio Gutiérrez, Lupe Juarez, Gilberto Gonzáles, and Clarencio Muñoz. (Courtesy of King Ranch Archives.)

This image is important to King Ranch baseball. Organized baseball required an umpire, and Luis Canales was in the thick of it at Assault Stadium, seen in the background. The park was named for Assault, the King Ranch horse that won the 1946 Triple Crown. The stadium was built by ranch employees, and it was said that attending a game there provided entertainment for even the less avid fans. They would gather on Sunday afternoons to barbecue, share stories of the week, and, of course, drink a few. (Courtesy of King Ranch Archives.)

This is a photograph of the 1961 King Ranch Cowboys. This was the last year of the team. Despite veteran players like Treviño, Buentello, and Borrego, the team could never really replace the leadership of Jesús Garza. The Cowboys saw newcomers, including the great-great-grandson of Richard King, the founder of the ranch, and Stephen Kleberg. In the Cowboys' last year, they played a light season and fielded several different lineups. Posing here are, from left to right, (first row) Nano Borrego, Abundio Rodríguez, Rene Villareal, Chino Rodríguez, Stephen Kleberg, Valentine Quintanilla, and Fernando Rodríguez; (second row) Antonio Rodríguez, Julián Buentello Jr., Cipriano Escobedo, Jesús García Jr., Raul Buentello, and Rene Borrego; (third row) Alberto Treviño, Alberto Buentello, David Borrego Sr., Raul Rodríguez, Chito Mendietta, and Coche Buentello. (Courtesy of King Ranch Archives.)

4

COLLEGE BALL

In Texas, Mexican Americans have always seen baseball as part of their environment and as an opportunity to advance their careers and education. What follows is a collection of players at Pan American College, which today is known as University of Texas–Pan American.

Pan American College was a trailblazer in opening the door to Latino and Mexican American players, many of whom had great careers as collegiate baseball players. Often, Mexican American players were the only minorities on their teams, but that did not stop them from producing both on the field and in the academic arena. Many of the following players have been inducted into the Rio Grande Valley Sports Hall of Fame or their university or college hall of fame. Not only did these men and women continue their love for the game after their collegiate careers, including playing professional and semipro baseball and softball—they contributed immensely to their communities as leaders, politicians, social activists, historians, and teachers of the game to a new generation. For many players, the game of baseball was a training facility for leadership, social consciousness, and duty to one's community.

Mexican Americans became part of the first baseball team at Edinburg College, known today as the University of Texas–Pan American. The first team included Mexican Americans such as Guerra and Chávez. The following year, 1929, the team was captained by Max Cavazos and included G. Garza, ? Pérez, and J. Pérez. The college and university baseball team would continue to be home to many Mexican American players.

Pitchers and catchers for Pan American College pose in 1956. They are, from left to right, (first row) Garsez, R. Wilshire, Aleios, and Garza; (second row) Flores, García, Chapa, W. Wilshire, and Valdez. Not pictured is Ruben Canche.

In the 1950s, Mexican Americans became leaders on the diamond. Here, pitcher Reynaldo Chapa (left) stands with catcher David Mosqueda, cocaptain of the Pan American College (University of Texas–Pan American) baseball team in 1956 and 1957. In 1993, Mosqueda was inducted into the Rio Grande Valley Sports Hall of Fame for his contributions as a baseball player and his role in officiating sports in Texas.

If anyone can be called "Mr. Baseball," it is Rene Torres, who played center field for Pan American College from 1965 to 1969. Torres, a scholar of all South Texas sports, has single-handedly recovered the history of baseball on the Texas borderlands. He has served his community as a member of the Texas Southmost College Board of Trustees, leading the Hispanic Serving Institution to a new road. Others can only hope to affect the world as Torres has.

Arnoldo Álvarez played baseball for Pan American College between 1967 and 1970. The Brownsville, Texas, native played the infield for the Broncos. Álvarez is the only man to be part of the University Interscholastic League state tournament both as a player and a coach. In 1965, he played third base for Brownsville Hanna High School and was a coach with Mercedes High School in 1974.

Felipe Leal pitched for Pan American College between 1963 and 1965 and was named National Association of Intercollegiate Athletics All-American in 1963 and 1964. Leal pitched a no-hitter in 1963 against Trinity University and ranks as one of the top pitchers in program history. In his career, Leal threw 248.1 innings and posted a 1.92 career ERA. He struck out 107 batters in one season and 20 batters in one game (1963). Leal played for both the Baltimore Orioles and California Angels.

Tony Barbosa Jr. pitched for Pan American College between 1967 and 1970, becoming the first hurler in program history to beat the University of Texas–Austin. Barbosa had a great college career, finishing with many records: 290 innings pitched, 351 strikeouts, a career 1.24 ERA, and an ERA of .89 in a season (1968). In 1969, as a National Collegiate Athletic Association All-American, he threw a no-hitter against the University of Houston. A year later, he tossed a one-hitter against Houston Baptist. Barbosa was drafted by the California Angels.

Camilo Rodríguez played third base for Pan American College between 1965 and 1967. The McAllen, Texas, native returned as an assistant coach in 1972. Following his playing days, he coached high school baseball and football at Sharyland, McAllen Rowe, and Mission Veterans, becoming a legend in South Texas. In 2002, he was inducted into the Rio Grande Valley Sports Hall of Fame for his coaching contributions.

Guadalupe Canul played basketball for Texas Southmost Junior College in 1960, becoming a National Junior College Athletic Association All-American, averaging 20 points and 20 rebounds per game. Canul pitched for Pan American College between 1963 and 1966, leading his team to its first postseason appearance. In 1964, Canul led the team with an 8-2 record. After his collegiate career on the hardwood and the pitching mound, Canul played 10 seasons in the Mexican Baseball League and became a semipro and high school coach.

Rudy Guajardo of Pharr, Texas, was a four-year letterman at Pan American College in the mid-1960s. Guajardo, a walk-on, earned a full scholarship and became the team's cocaptain with Luis Alamia. Considered an all-around player and team leader, Guajardo hit for average and power, had a great arm behind the plate, and, most important, was a true leader on and off the diamond.

Nieves Cortéz and his brother Richard Cortéz played for Pan American College in the 1960s. The Cortéz brothers led the Salazar Grocery All-Stars of Edinburg, Texas, to the National Baseball Congress World Series in Wichita, Kansas, in 1968. Major League players such as Tom Seaver, Dave Winfield, Don Sutton, Ozzie Smith, Roger Clemens, and Tony Gwynn played in the National Baseball Congress World Series.

Pan American became home not only to Mexican American players in the 1950s and 1960s, but also African American players. Murray Grant, a pitcher in 1957, was part of the Joe Davis Ginners semipro team that won the Texas World Series and advanced to the National Baseball Congress World Series in Wichita, Kansas, in 1963. In the above photograph, Grant is in the second row, third from left. The second African American to play baseball at Pan American College was Gary West (left), a centerfielder, in 1964.

Lupe Salinas played for Pan American College in 1970–1973 and is known for beating the University of Texas 1-0 in 1971, sending his team to the College World Series. Salinas was an NCAA All-American, finishing his career with many records that still stand today: a no-hitter in 1972 against St. Mary, a one-hitter in 1971 against Missouri, 41 complete games, 356.2 innings pitched, 1.16 career ERA, .39 ERA in a season (1972), and 309 strikeouts. Salinas is one of the best pitchers to ever come out of South Texas.

Héctor Salinas was born in Elsa, Texas, and became a great player at Pan American College. He also made huge contributions on the baseball diamond as a coach at the college level. Along with his teammate Tony Barbosa, Salinas became an NCAA All-American in 1967 for Pan American College. In 1993, Salinas was asked to bring baseball back to life at Texas A&M University–Kingsville. The school had been a trailblazer for Mexican American athletes and students since it opened its doors in 1926.

The 1965 Pan American College baseball team was one of the best in the history of the program. Shown here are, from left to right, (first row) Ruben Guajardo, Bucky Rodríguez, Joe Morales, Buddy Roberts, Jesús Luna, and Enrique Guerra; (second row) coach Chuck Young, Gary West, Frank Elguesaba, Héctor Salinas, Luis Alamia, Lupe Canul, Tommy Cook, and Felipe Leal.

The 1966 Pan American College team poses for a photograph. Shown are, from left to right, (first row) cocaptain Luis Alamia, head coach Larry Ensminger, and cocaptain Rudy Guajardo; (second row) Nieves Cortéz, Chuy Luna, Arnoldo Álvarez, Bucky Rodríguez, and Richard Alamia; (third row) Héctor Salinas, Johnnie Guzman, and Kiki Guerra; (fourth row) Larry Brown, Bill Lentz, and Greg Rodríguez.

The Alamias are the first family of the University of Texas Pan American baseball. Luis Alamia (right) and brother Richy (below) played in 1963. Luis "Prince of Thieves" Alamia Jr. started his college career at New Mexico Highlands University, where he hit .304 and broke the record for steals. At Pan American College, Luis stole 64 bases from 1963 to 1965. Richy earned his law degree from St. Mary's University.

Tommy Sandoval was a pitcher for Pan American College from 1967 to 1970, winning 20 games, pitching 241.2 innings, and throwing 193 strikeouts during his career. In 1970, he went 8-0 with a 1.45 ERA and was honored with the Lou Hassel Award for best male student athlete. In 2004, his family established the Tommy Sandoval Jr. Endowment Scholarship to benefit the University of Texas–Pan American baseball program.

Johnny Guzman, a San Antonio native, played for Cliff Gustafson at South San Antonio High School, winning state titles in 1963 and 1964. At Pan American College, Guzman was known as a composed pitcher who controlled all aspects of the game.

Johnny Guzman was honored with the Lou Hassel Award for best senior male student athlete in the spring of 1969. The award is given to an athlete who exhibits and maintains excellence both on the field and in academics.

Pan American College's first baseball team after World War II took the field in 1948. The team played only ten games, eight of them conference games. On the schedule were games against Blinn Junior College, Laredo Junior College, Uvalde Junior College, and Seguin Junior College. Players on the first postwar team included Marburger, Aguirre, Ely, Johnson, Smith, Jennings, Riskind, Sandoval, Molina, Balusek, Martínez, Garza, Heimlich, Hottel, S. Solís, H. Solís, Salinas, and Cavazos.

Pictured here are, from left to right, Pan America College 1959 team leaders Oakley Davidson, Manny Saenz, Sonny Paz, and Coach Connor. Saenz was voted the team's best all-around player. He pitched a two-hitter against St. Mary's in 1959. Paz was known by his teammates as the "fireman" because of his control on the pitching mound. He was named the teammate with the best team spirit in 1959.

The Pan American College 1978 women's softball team poses for a photograph. From left to right are (first row) Polly Paulit, Paula Martínez, Melba Llanes, Kathy Garza, and Josie Ayala; (second row) coach Kelly Bass, Noelia Villarreal, Shirly James, Cindy Treviño, Bertha Chavana, and Gloria Benavidez. Softball has been part of South Texas since the 1930s. Pilar García of Brownsville was one of the best and most-loved semipro fast-pitch aces. She led a team dedicated to the Brownsville Public Health Nursing Association and their milk fund against Dorfman, the fast-pitch league champions, in 1939 at the 36th Diamond. The nursing organization served underprivileged children.

South Texas women's semipro fast-pitch teams continued during the World War II era. Teams included Dorfman Jewelers, Texas Simpson Clippers, Packard Clippers, Brownsville High School, Pan American Ladies, and Fort Brown Women. Softball was part of the vibrant sports scene in the Lower Rio Grande Valley.

Faustino Cavazos was a power hitter for the 1960 Pan American College team. Here, Cavazos hits a game-ending three-run home run that allowed Humberto Taddei and Chip Zamora to score.

The 1960 Pan American College team went 14-11 and included Richie Flores, who played right field and pitched. Flores (pictured) hit for a .394 average, and in 1962, pitched a one-hitter against Corpus Christi. He was voted outstanding player of the year. Other players on the team included Eraslio Flores, Reynaldo Contreras, Lino Arrevalo, Oakley Davidson, Humberto Taddei, Chip Zamora, Manuel Saenz, Adolfo Salinas, Esasilo Villarreal, Faustino Cavazos, Art Henkel, Ruben Farias, Sony Paz, Larry Morris, and Carlos Ortiz.

5

THE LONE STAR STATE

At the conclusion of the 2014 TD Ameritrade College Home Run Derby, viewers may have been surprised that the final participants were both from South Texas: Texas Tech University's Eric Gutiérrez and the University of Texas's Tres Barrera. After all, Mexican American athletes have seldom garnered major attention in such national events. Barrera outslugged his former high school teammate in the finals (25 to 18) to claim the title. This event provided a hint of the ability and history of this ethnic group's ties to baseball in the Lone Star State. Gutiérrez and Barrera are the most recent in a long line of peloteros who have competed on diamonds throughout Texas over the past century and more. The photographs in this chapter provide but a sense of the breadth and depth of this history. The chapter touches on various regions, from deep South Texas, west to Lubbock and San Angelo, and to the Houston area. The photographs depict not only athletic talent, but the utilization of sport for the development and sustenance of communal and ethnic ties.

Wherever individuals of this background ventured, *la pelota* was a part of daily life, especially on Sundays. Participants played at all levels. Many Mexican Americans played for semipro and professional teams (some even signed with major-league organizations), as well as in community leagues. As more and more *atletas* managed to remain in high school (and even college) after World War II, it became possible to represent hometowns in interscholastic competition. At first, most played for local institutions, such as Pan American and Southwest Texas State Colleges in the 1950s and 1960s. Many of these *pioneros* played well, earned college degrees, and, after graduation, became pillars of communities, both within and outside Texas. It is such players who helped make it possible for current-day athletes like Gutiérrez and Barrera to make a splash at the national level. The future of Mexican Americans and baseball in Texas appear as bright and as significant as ever.

Sonny Benavidez played for the College Station, Texas, White Sox Little League team in 1957. He also played four years of baseball at Consolidated High School (1960–1964). During his high school days, Benavidez's woodshop teacher was also his baseball coach. The student asked his coach to order five wood blocks from the Louisville Slugger bat factory in Kentucky. Benavidez then proceeded to use woodshop equipment to make five bats for the team, one of which is shown in this photograph. He retired from the Federal Bureau of Investigation. (Courtesy of Sonny Benavidez.)

The Bluebirds were based in San Ygnacio, Texas, and played throughout the southern parts of the Lone Star State. The team continued to play until 1942, when most of its players joined the armed forces. For example, Chano Rodríguez served in Gen. George Patton's 3rd Army. Shown here are, from left to right, (first row) Arturo Benavidez, Lalo Solís, Manuel Boteo, José Luis Torres, Alonso Uribe, Nalo Benavidez, and Julián Solís; (second row) Tino Solís, José Lerma, Blas Maria Uribe, Chencho Benavidez, Romeo Uribe, and Chano Rodríguez. (Courtesy of Dr. Cruz C. Torres.)

This announcement was for a contest between the Zapata Cubs and Almanco. These teams were part of a winter league based in the Rio Grande Valley in the 1950s and into the 1960s. Almanco was one of several teams that were based in Mexico that competed in this association. (Courtesy of Dr. Cruz C. Torres.)

This team was organized in 1957 by Zapata County sheriff C.M. Hein. The Hawks were a semipro team. The 1958 area championship team poses here. The members are, from left to right, (first row) Roberto Cuellar, Ramiro Torres, Homero Espinoza, Mario Flores, and Gilberto Davila; (second row) Leobardo Benavidez, Sheriff Hein, "Borado" Garza, Rodolfo Espinoza, Luis Martínez, Jorge González, and "Beto" Tamez. Despite Hein's German surname, he was *puro* Mexican American. (Courtesy of Dr. Cruz C. Torres.)

Winter Base - Ball
LEAGUE GAME
Sunday Nov. 10, 1957

HIGH SCHOOL FIELD
Zapata, Texas

ZAPATA CUBS vs ALMANCO

LINE - UPS

Torres	C.F.	Mata	2B
Martinez	2B	D. York	R.F.
Hein	R.F.	Uribe	3B
Tamez	R.F.	Sanchez	CF
R. Espinosa	S.S.	Flores	SS
L. Benavides	1B	Idrogo	1B
H. Espinosa	C	Luna	C
M. Flores	3B	Gonzalez	LF
M. Medina Jr.	P.	R. Reyna Rodriguez	
G. Davila			
T. Lopez			
A. Espinosa			
R. Cuellar			

UTILITIES: ZAPATA

L. Martinez Jr., J. Gonzalez, A. Vela, C. Morales, Rene Sanchez

Adults 35c - Children 10c

Ramiro Torres, a longtime entrepreneur from Zapata, Texas, was also very much involved in promoting baseball in the region. His father was one of the original Bluebirds. Here, Torres stands next to his father's uniform. Starting in the late 1950s, Torres was instrumental in putting together another notable team from this region, the Zapata Lakers. The Lakers, unaffiliated with any league, would barnstorm the region, playing against squads from San Antonio and McAllen. (Courtesy of Dr. Cruz C. Torres.)

The Zapata Lakers were organized by Ramiro Torres in 1959 and barnstormed throughout southern Texas and into Mexico. The squad, which included players from the semipro, collegiate, and high school ranks, traveled and played between the months of April and September. The Lakers never had a losing season, playing as many as 40 games in a campaign. The team finally disbanded in the 1970s. (Courtesy of Dr. Cruz C. Torres.)

Ramon Cantu was a leading promoter of Mexican American baseball teams and leagues in the Rio Grande Valley. He was inducted into the Rio Grande Valley Sports Hall of Fame in 1995. Cantu was the promoter and manager of a team based in Edinburg that dominated play in the region in the late 1950s and into the 1960s. (Courtesy of Dr. Juan Coronado and Vicente and Francisco Estévis.)

Tommie Encinas (first row, center) played for the Waco, Texas, Pirates in 1948. The year before, he played with the Pittsburgh Pirates' minor-league team, the Uniontown Coal Barons, in Pennsylvania. He later played for the Eagles of Mexcali, Mexico, a Pirates affiliate in the Class C Southwest International League. Encinas, raised in the Pomona Valley in California, played military ball and was a medic in the Pacific during World War II. Many California ballplayers signed to professional contracts started their careers in the Texas leagues as early as the 1920s. (Courtesy of the Encinas family.)

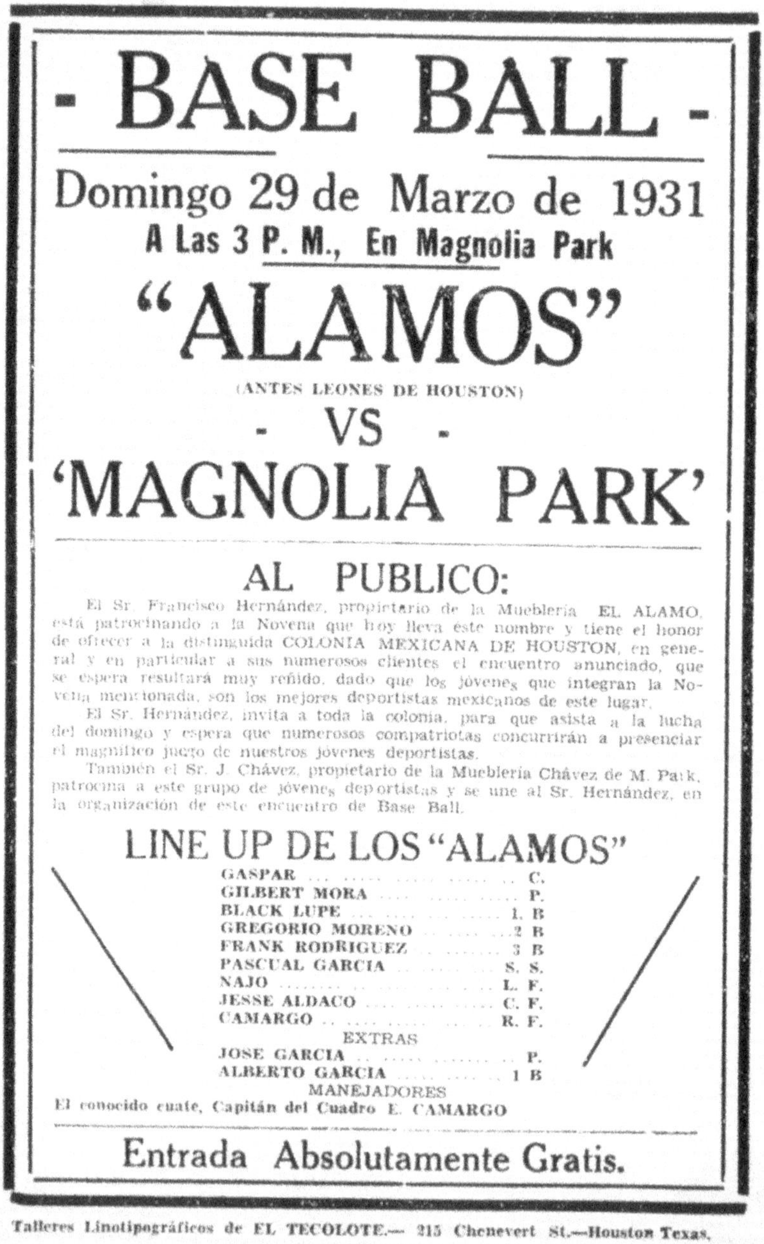

- BASE BALL -

Domingo 29 de Marzo de 1931
A Las 3 P. M., En Magnolia Park

"ALAMOS"

(ANTES LEONES DE HOUSTON)

- VS -

'MAGNOLIA PARK'

AL PUBLICO:

El Sr. Francisco Hernández, propietario de la Muebleria EL ALAMO, está patrocinando a la Novena que hoy lleva este nombre y tiene el honor de ofrecer a la distinguida COLONIA MEXICANA DE HOUSTON, en general y en particular a sus numerosos clientes el encuentro anunciado, que se espera resultará muy reñido, dado que los jóvenes que integran la Novena mencionada, son los mejores deportistas mexicanos de este lugar.

El Sr. Hernández, invita a toda la colonia, para que asista a la lucha del domingo y espera que numerosos compatriotas concurrirán a presenciar el magnifico juego de nuestros jóvenes deportistas.

También el Sr. J. Chávez, propietario de la Muebleria Chávez de M. Park, patrocina a este grupo de jóvenes deportistas y se une al Sr. Hernández, en la organización de este encuentro de Base Ball.

LINE UP DE LOS "ALAMOS"

GASPAR	C.
GILBERT MORA	P.
BLACK LUPE	1. B
GREGORIO MORENO	2 B
FRANK RODRIGUEZ	3 B
PASCUAL GARCIA	S. S.
NAJO	L. F.
JESSE ALDACO	C. F.
CAMARGO	R. F.

EXTRAS

JOSE GARCIA	P.
ALBERTO GARCIA	1 B

MANEJADORES

El conocido cuate, Capitán del Cuadro E. CAMARGO

Entrada Absolutamente Gratis.

Talleres Linotipográficos de EL TECOLOTE.— 215 Chenevert St.—Houston Texas.

The city of Houston has an extraordinary baseball history dating back to at least the 1920s. One of the most famous teams was the Alamos, formerly known as the Leones de Houston (Houston Lions). The team was sponsored by a furniture store, El Alamo. The owner, Francisco Hernández, along with other business leaders, sponsored and promoted baseball throughout Houston. This handbill for a game in March 1931 includes the lineup for the Alamos. (Courtesy of the Houston Metropolitan Research Center, Houston Public Library, the Mexican American Family and Photograph Collection.)

This Houston team was sponsored by the Mexican Inn in 1934. Mexican and Mexican American businesses were the economic foundation of teams and players. Many large communities, including San Antonio, Corpus Christi, and Houston, established Spanish-speaking business groups to promote economic independence from the larger society. Several business leaders had played ball in Mexico and Texas and used their financial clout to promote teams, which in turn encouraged fans to purchase their products. (Courtesy of the Houston Metropolitan Research Center, Houston Public Library, the Mexican American Family and Photograph Collection.)

Leo "Najo" Alanis—born in Mexico, but growing up in Mission—was an accomplished player in local leagues, playing with the Mission-based Treinta-Treinta club and also in Mexico until 1926. He eventually signed with the San Antonio Missions and had a spring-training tryout with the Chicago White Sox. Unfortunately, he broke his leg in July 1926 and never again had a chance to make the big leagues. He remained active as a player and manager in southern Texas until the late 1950s. (Courtesy of Dr. Juan Coronado.)

In addition to baseball, Houston's Mexican American community formed several softball teams, including this 1944 Second Ward Merchant's team. As with baseball, softball teams were sponsored by Spanish-speaking businesses. Merchants purchased uniforms and equipment, maintained fields, and provided transportation for away games. Larger businesses attracted the best players because of economic incentives, including monetary rewards for outstanding games. (Courtesy of the Houston Metropolitan Research Center, Houston Public Library, the Mexican American Family and Photograph Collection.)

The 1967 National Baseball Congress state championship took place in Lubbock, Texas. Shown here is the Salazar Grocery Semi-Pro Baseball Team of Edinburg, Texas, which won the state title that year. The team had won the championship in 1963 under its previous name, the Edinburg Davis Ginners. Ramon Cantu, known as "Mr. Baseball" in the Rio Grande Valley region, was a local entrepreneur who helped put this team together. (Courtesy of Dr. Juan Coronado and Vicente and Francisco Estévis.)

Like many Texas ballplayers, John Ysidro Dickinson also played in Mexico. It was not unusual for Mexican Americans to play six months in the United States and six months in Mexico. The best Mexican American ballplayers were heavily recruited by Mexican teams, especially outstanding hitters and pitchers. Dickinson (second row, third from right) played for several Mexican teams in the 1940s and 1950s. Mexican American ballplayers from California, Arizona, and New Mexico also played ball on both sides of the border. (Courtesy of John Y. Dickinson III.)

The Crumbie team played in the West Side Little League in El Paso in the early 1950s. Crumbie, a food-distribution company, was just one of several local businesses that sponsored clubs. Armando "Muggins" Ruiz (first row, fourth from left) played second base for this 1951 team. He later played American Legion ball and then went on to a long career as a counselor in local schools and at El Paso Community College. (Courtesy of Armando "Muggins" Ruiz.)

Members of the 1927 Laredo High School baseball team are seen here. Among these players was Rogelio García (first row, third from left), who went on to success as a shortstop for his alma mater. He played semiprofessional baseball with a Laredo squad in the 1930s. In his high school yearbook, García was referred to as "the best shortstop the High School has ever known." The Laredo semipro nine often played against teams from northern Mexico. (Courtesy of Juan Senties Jr.)

Charlie Sierra (far right) played for the Boston Red Sox farm team in El Paso in 1947 and 1948 in the Class C Arizona-Texas League. Charlie's father, Ernesto, was an outstanding player in Arizona. Ernesto traveled to Texas, playing baseball in the 1920s. He moved his family to East Los Angeles. Charlie and his brother Ernie signed contracts with the Boston Red Sox. During World War II, Ernie flew 25 bombing missions over Germany. Charlie played military ball in the Air Force in the early 1950s. (Courtesy of Charlie Sierra.)

THE LONE STAR STATE

The Laredo Apaches were part of the Gulf Coast League from 1951 to 1953. The circuit consisted of teams in Brownsville, Corpus Christi, Harlingen, Port Arthur, and Texas City in Texas, and Lake Charles in Louisiana. Here, Juan Senties holds up his batting-title trophy for hitting .379 in the last year of the league's existence. The team's final record that year was a mediocre 71-76. (Courtesy of Juan Senties Jr.)

Juan Senties followed a very unusual path to professional baseball. The Veracruz native was attending medical school in Mexico when he was given the chance to play professionally for a border team, the Nuevo Laredo Tecolotes. He left behind his studies in the late 1940s, and major-leaguer Beto Avila recruited him to play in the Gulf Coast League in Texas. In this photograph, he wears the uniform of a minor-league team in Wichita, Kansas. (Courtesy of Juan Senties Jr.)

Baseball in Texas drew huge crowds, especially on Sundays. Hundreds, sometimes thousands of fans filled stadiums throughout the Lone Star State. The ball field was a cultural and political hub. The diamond was where the community came to cheer its favorite team and boo the opposing players, but it was also an arena where politics was discussed, labor strategies were formulated, and money was raised for campaigns and lawsuits. The ballpark was also where people registered to vote, citizenship information was distributed, union dues were collected, war bonds were sold, and announcements were made of economic boycotts of specific downtown businesses that refused to serve Mexican Americans. (Courtesy of the Raphael and Virginia Galván Papers, Texas A&M University, Corpus Christi.)

THE LONE STAR STATE

Inspired by the players in the All-American Girls Professional Baseball League, Las Estrellas was the first all-female baseball team in the Lubbock, Texas, area, starting in 1950. The team played through 1953. They came together, in part, to provide a diversion for a recently widowed friend. The trucks that players rode in to get to nearby towns and play other Latinas were often the same vehicles they used to work the area's cotton fields. As seen here, living members of the squad gathered in Lubbock for a reunion in 2009. (Courtesy of *Latino Lubbock*.)

The Osos was a team that played in West Texas during the 1920s. One resident recalled that the squad was one of several that crisscrossed this part of the state. Games were a cause for celebration and often included bands, dances, and meals. During the Great Depression, the teams began to die out as the harsh economic circumstances made it necessary for players and their families to leave the area of San Angelo. (Courtesy of Southwest Collection Archive, Texas Tech University.)

The Guadalupe Sombreros pose in the 1940s. This youth team hailed from the mostly Mexican American barrio in the northern section of Lubbock, Texas. (Courtesy of the Southwest Collection Archive, Texas Tech University.)

The Bryan, Texas, Aztecas were one of several teams established by the Mexican American community since the 1940s. Several great players have come out of Bryan and nearby College Station. One of the first was Homer Thomas Martínez, a three-year letterman with the Aggies baseball team. Manuel García graduated from Consolidated High School in 1956, lettering in baseball for four years and being named MVP. García returned to his former high school as the head coach. (Courtesy of Lionel García.)

Camilo Estévis is pictured in the uniform of the 1961 Southern Association (AA) Atlanta Crackers. He pitched for this team for one season and had a 5-5 record. He was later promoted to the Albuquerque Dukes (affiliated with the Dodgers) and traded to the White Sox organization. He did not reach the majors, and completed his professional career in 1967 after having played two years in the Mexican League. (Courtesy of Dr. Juan Coronado and Vicente and Francisco Estévis.)

Armando De León (left) and his brother Arnoldo (right), pose proudly in their Little League uniforms around 1957. In the background are the cotton pickers' quarters where the large De León family lived. At that young age, the Robtown, Texas, siblings worked the nearby fields during summers along with their father, Jesús. The boys would work from 7:00 a.m. to 6:00 p.m. and then go play Little League ball in town. As adults, both enjoyed successful professional careers. (Courtesy of Julia De León.)

1956 - Rene Torres, batboy

The Brownsville Regals participated in the very competitive Rio Grande Valley Semi-Pro League in 1956. The circuit comprised teams from throughout the valley, including San Benito, three squads from Harlingen, Weslaco, Pharr, and Edinburg. The Regals matured into a solid group with a pitching staff comparable to any Class C professional team. The batboy in this photograph grew up to be a significant figure in valley baseball. (Courtesy of Rene Torres.)

On Sundays, farm hands such as these would brush aside field work and turn their energies toward beating the competition, generally teams visiting from nearby farms or towns. The weekend event attracted ex-players, teenagers practicing the art of courting, school children, and those wanting to learn the latest *chisme* (gossip). The camaraderie of the game led to strong group bonds—several in this photograph of the Chapman Ranch Steers became *compadres*. While the occasion reinforced ethnicity, it also acted to Americanize those present. Jesús De León is at far right. (Courtesy of Julia De León.)

This poster promotes a 1932 contest between an all-star team from Monterrey, Mexico, and the local nine from Laredo at Liberty Park. Among the players was Rogelio García, who had been a star shortstop for Laredo High School. Unfortunately, Rogelio's career was cut short when he passed away at the young age of 30. (Courtesy of Juan Senties Jr.)

BASE-BALL
Liberty Park—2 p. m.
SENSACIONALES JUEGOS
Domingo 28 de Febrero
—1932—
JUEGOS INTERNACIONALES!

Monterrey "All Stars"
—vs—
LAREDOS

Al Penasco—La potente novena "All Stars" de Monterrey, está compuesta de jugadores escogidos de la metropoli del norte. Fausto, Moreno, y Flores es un trio de formidables bateadores. Sotero Villarreal el "as" de los pitchers de Monterrey "All Stars" con su formidable batería que trae al pie, tiene la seguridad de llevarse los honores.

La novena de Laredo está compuesta de los más importantes elementos beisboleros locales; como Sixto Barrera, Kelo, Pelos, Boca, Muñoz, Rubio, Davalina, Etc. La ciudad de Laredo puede sentirse orgullosa al contar con una novena de primera magnitud en nuestro medio. Los muchachos que componen el Team Laredo deseosos de dar al público en su inauguración lo mejor de su repertorio, tienen tres semanas de estar entrenándose debidamente para dar al público en su primer juego lo mejor de la temporada en Laredo.

—— LINE-UP ——

MONTERREY "ALL STARS"		"LAREDOS"
Jose Santos	Catcher	Boca y Salinas
Sotero Villarreal, Gumesindo Martinez	Pitcher	Rubio, Davalina, Villarreal
Agustin Gonzalez	1a Base	Sheffield
Genaro Fausto	2a Base	Pelos y Juarez
Carlos Narvaez	3a Base	Sixto Barrera
Jesus Salas	S. S.	Kelo Garcia
Alfredo Flores	R. F.	Pinita
Galeno Flores	C. F.	Muñoz
Domingo Moreno	L. F.	Chevo
	Sub	Guetierrez

PRECIOS DE ENTRADA:
ADULTOS 30c   JOVENES HASTA 14 AÑOS 10c   NIÑOS 5c
DAMAS GRATIS

NOTA:—Habrá Servicio Especial de Tranvias del Centro de la Ciudad al Park Liberty y de Regreso Tambien.

ALDAPE PRINTING CO.

Individuals of Mexicano/Mexican American backgrounds have been playing baseball along the border of southern Texas for more than 100 years. This photograph of an unidentified team is from the mid-to-late 1910s and is among the oldest evidence documenting such participation encountered during the authors' research for this project. (Courtesy of Dr. Juan Coronado and Vicente and Francisco Estévis.)

This 1953 Victoria Eagles team is a later version of the Eagles, featuring a mostly Mexican American squad. The squad included two "whites," competing in a local "Mexican" institution. (Courtesy of Professor Ed Byerly and Frank Ortiz.)

John Ysidro Dickinson (right) was born in Laredo, Texas, in 1908 and played ball for the majority of his 88 years in South Texas and Mexico. He played against several major-league stars when they barnstormed through the Laredo area, including Jimmie Foxx, Dixie Walker, and Mickey Cochrane. He pitched against Dizzy Dean when Dean was stationed at Fort Sam Houston in San Antonio. Dickinson also played several years on various teams in Mexico. He eventually became a certified public accountant in the United States and Mexico. (Courtesy of John Y. Dickinson III.)

Eric Gutiérrez played varsity at Sharyland High School for four years, earning all-state and first team all-district his senior year. He was named MVP of his district as a senior. Despite these accomplishments, Texas Tech was the only Division I school to offer Gutiérrez a scholarship. He rewarded Tech's investment in him by helping lead the school to its first trip to the College World Series in 2014. (Courtesy of Texas Tech University Athletics.)

Eric Gutiérrez crushes one of his 52 home runs at the 2014 College Baseball Home Run Derby at Rosenblatt Stadium in Omaha, Nebraska. Gutiérrez was joined in the finals by a former teammate from Sharyland High School, Tres Barrera, who now plays for the University of Texas. While Gutiérrez hit more home runs overall, Barrera outslugged him in the finals 25-18 to win the championship. (Courtesy of Texas Tech University Athletics.)

Seen here are Camilo Estévis, who hails from Edinburg, and his collegiate coach at both Pan American College and New Mexico Highlands University, John Donnelly. Estévis signed with the Dodgers organization after playing at NMHU. He is seen here as a member of the Albuquerque Dukes, being honored by the team. Estévis asked his former coach to share in the spotlight. Donnelly helped many valley youths attend college through baseball scholarships. (Courtesy of Dr. Juan Coronado and Vicente and Francisco Estévis.)

This press release from New Mexico Highlands University announces Camilo Estévis's signing with the Los Angeles Dodgers organization. The document indicates that the team noticed Estévis's talents not only at the collegiate level, but also through his successful play with various valley-area semiprofessional teams, such as the Davis Ginners and the McAllen Dons. Estévis had previously turned down offers from the Pirates and other clubs in order to complete his education at NMHU, where he earned a degree in physical education and Spanish. (Courtesy of Dr. Juan Coronado and Vicente and Francisco Estévis.)

New Mexico Highlands University
Las Vegas, New Mexico
Sports Information

EDWARD J. GROTH
Director

May 10, 1960

FOR RELEASE THURSDAY, MAY 12

LAS VEGAS, N. M.——The world champion Los Angeles Dodgers baseball organization has announced signing of New Mexico Highlands University's ace righthander Camilo Estevis to a pro contract.

Estevis, an All-Frontier hurler for the past two years and the number one strikeout artist in the nation according to latest NAIA statistics, will report to Atlanta of the Double A Southern Association on June 5. He is a senior here at Highlands University and his reporting date comes at the end of the spring quarter.

The 6-4 senior was signed by scout Floyd Patterson on the Highlands campus for "a sizeable bonus". Patterson scouted Estevis at the annual Frontier Conference championships last week and watched him shutout Panhandle A&M College 4-0 on a three hitter.

"We have been watching Estevis for the past two years," said Patterson. "He was scouted in Wichita, Kansas, last season when he pitched for McAllen, Texas, in the National Baseball Congress and several times this season," he added.

As a college pitcher, Estevis has posted a four-year pitching record of 31 wins against six losses. He started his college career with Pan-American College in Edinburgh, Texas, and then transfered to Highlands University. Over the past three seasons, Estevis has turned down offers from the Pittsburgh organization, Kansas City Athletics, the Boston Red Sox, and Corpus Christi and San Antonio of the Texas League.   (more)

This photograph of men at work and play was given to Héctor Solíz by an older woman from his hometown of Encinal, a tiny community about 39 miles north of Laredo. The men have never been identified. The picture, however, was taken in South Texas during the Depression, and the men appear to be employed under the auspices of one of President Roosevelt's employment programs, the Works Project Administration. (Courtesy of Héctor Solíz.)

This program insert is from a game featuring major-league all-stars competing in an exhibition contest against an all-star team comprised exclusively from the Rio Grande Valley region. Among the notables from this area to play in the 1957 or 1958 contest were two of the Estévis brothers. The local squad was managed by another area legend, Leo "Najo" Alanis, from Mission. (Courtesy of Dr. Juan Coronado and Vicente and Francisco Estévis.)

This is a baseball team from Benavides in Duval County. Second from left in the second row is Coach E.C. Lerma, one of the first and most successful Mexican American high school coaches in the state of Texas. Even though he made his mark primarily as a football coach (starting in 1940), he also coached other sports at Benavides High School, including track and basketball. He even had some time to play baseball with other Mexican Americans in his community. (Courtesy of Armando González.)

6

COAST TO COAST

The first three decades of the 20th century witnessed unprecedented movement of Mexicans into the United States, fanning out to nearly every state of the nation. Mexicans left their native country due, in large part, to class warfare, open conflict between the government and the church, and the great demand for labor in the United States. These major events in Mexico coincided with both the emergence of the United States as a world power, especially after World War I, and the growth of capitalism at home. Each individual and family that left Mexico would eventually experience major social, economic, and political obstacles. Nevertheless, they shared a common destiny and charted untold dramas and remarkable achievements in order to survive in a new country. With the mutual assistance of Mexican Americans who had roots dating to before the arrival of the *Mayflower*, these newcomers took the first steps to develop stable communities and become a permanent sector of the working class.

No matter where they settled, Mexicans, and their Mexican American brothers and sisters, elaborately choreographed social, cultural, and political infrastructures. Sadly, these first two generations are almost gone from the physical landscape of our nation. Their collective wealth of timeless memories and great stories nearly disappeared with them, but the extraordinary efforts of community historians and university scholars saved this rich history via interviews and documentation. In this way, their rightful place within the true history of the United States has been retained.

This chapter reveals that Mexicans and Mexican Americans formed baseball and softball teams and leagues over a century ago. Community leaders saw baseball as both a recreational experience and a catalyst for social and political change. While this chapter looks at several states, two regions are highlighted. The first region is the Central Valley in California, which runs along Highway 99 from Sacramento to Bakersfield, including the city of Stockton. Mexicans and Mexican Americans worked largely in the agricultural fields. The second region, the Rocky Mountain states of Colorado, Wyoming, and Montana, along with Nebraska, witnessed Mexicans and Mexican Americans working in the sugar-beet industry. In both of these regions, Mexicans and Mexican Americans established outstanding teams and produced incredible players.

David and Carlos Salazar are seen here in 1961, when they umpired for several California Little Leagues, including Central Pasadena, East Pasadena, and San Marino, in the 1960s and 1970s. David (left) played at Muir Junior College in 1950–1951 and for Los Angeles State College in 1953–1954. He played military ball while serving in Japan with the 40th Division, 225th Regiment. Carlos (right), an outstanding player, began umpiring in 1969 and still umpires high school and college baseball and softball, high school football, and volleyball. (Courtesy of Carlos Salazar.)

The 1955 Babe Ruth League playoffs took place at Gilmore Field, the home of the Pacific Coast League Hollywood Stars. Mark Scott (center) was the Stars broadcaster and, for many years, the voice of Home Run Derby. To his left is Phil Chelvig, and to his right is Carlos Salazar. The Pasadena team, led by Salazar, lost to Oakland 4-3. The winner went on to Plainview, Texas, for the Babe Ruth World Series. Salazar started playing ball with the Pasadena Baseball School at Brookside Park, playing at the age of 10 on professional-sized fields. (Courtesy of Carlos Salazar.)

The Pasadena Community College team were cochampions in 1958 and 1959. This 1959 squad had at least four Mexican Americans: Ray Padilla (first row, second from right), Manuel Venegas (first row, fourth from right), Hank Pérez (second row, fourth from left), and Carlos Salazar (second row, second from right). Padilla graduated from Montebello High School, Venegas later played ball at Los Angeles State College, Pérez played at Cathedral High School, and Salazar was an outstanding pitcher and first baseman for John Muir High School. (Courtesy of Carlos Salazar.)

The California Mexican League was established in 1954. Among its early organizers were Jesús Valverde, Ray and Tubby Álvarez, Rubén Lemon, Del Ortega, and Primo and Sachus Orozco. Several teams were formed, including this 1958 Stockton Latin American Club (LAC). From left to right are (front) unidentified batboy; (first row) Ben Nicolas, Joe Cortéz, John Sánchez, Mel Núñez, unidentified, John Álvarez, and Manny Juárez; (second row) Bob Álvarez, Gene Nelson, Jim Reynoso, Don Stevens, unidentified, Bill Stevens, Larry Burgess, and John A. Cardona. (Courtesy of John A. Cardona.)

The Stockton Latin American Club won the California Mexican League Championship in 1959. Posing here are, from left to right, (front) unidentified batboy; (first row) Joe Cortéz, Alfred Del Plato, Ben Guerrero, Manny Juárez, John Álvarez, and Bill Stevens; (second row) LAC athletic director John A. Cardona, Gene Nelson, Ernie Guerrero, Ben Nicolas, unidentified, Don Stevens, Larry Burgess, and unidentified. Other league teams included Merced, Modesto, Sacramento, Woodland, and Tracy. (Courtesy of John A. Cardona.)

The LAC won the California Mexican League Championship again in 1964. Shown here are, from left to right, (first row) Trini Ruiz, Pete Tovar, unidentified, Joe Aguilar, Carl Agabuls, and batboy Joey Aguilar; (second row) Bob Ross, unidentified, Joe Peña, two unidentified, and Tino Cuevas. (Courtesy of John A. Cardona.)

This 1932 Mexican American Stockton team was known as El Club Charro. From left to right are (first row) Bill Martínez, Manuel Gonzáles, Fred Ávila, Paul Morones, Jimmie Martínez, and Johnnie Martínez; (second row) Pete Sandos, Johnny Ávila, Lottie Herrera, Fidencio Herrera, Roy Álvarez, and Raymond Muñoz. Álvarez's son Roy Jr. played and managed ball for many years around Stockton, Modesto, and Tracy. (Courtesy of Roy Álvarez Jr.)

Club Azteca, a powerhouse throughout the Central Valley, was one of several outstanding teams from the city of Stockton. Seen here are, from left to right, (first row) A. Sánchez, S. Conterio, J. Bernardo, batboy C. Álvarez, Matt Wilson, ? Cocoran, and R. Álvarez Jr.; (second row) R. Álvarez, Gil Granados, Daymon Cook, ? Roth, J. Naraha, J. Aguilar, R. Laughlin, and manager T. Álvarez. Mexican American teams were allowed to carry four non–Mexican Americans on their rosters. (Courtesy of Roy Álvarez Jr.)

The Pan American team of Stockton is seen here in the 1950s. From left to right are (first row) unidentified and batboy Roy Álvarez III; (second row) John Bernardo, John ?, Julie Hernández, and Steve Axt; (third row) Henry Sánchez, Bernie Mack, Paul Olivet, ? Frank, Rafael Rodríguez, Jess Coverubilas, and manager Roy Álvarez Jr. (Courtesy of Roy Álvarez Jr.)

The Stockton team México is seen here in 1930. This was Stockton's first organized team of Mexican players. The team played throughout the Central San Joaquin Valley. Ralph S. Valverde (second row, center) organized and managed the México team. He was born in 1898 in Encinilla, Chihuahua, Mexico. From left to right are (first row) unidentified, Pete Hernández, and Lottie Herrera; (second row) Jess Hernández, Tino Valverde, Ralph S. Valverde, John Ávila, and unidentified; (third row) unidentified, Jesús Valverde, Leo Hernández, unidentified, and Fidel Hernández. (Courtesy of Louis A. Valverde.)

Jesús "Sue" Valverde was born in 1910 in Mexico. With his widowed mother and 11 brothers and sisters, the family settled in Stockton, California, in 1920. Jesús attended St. Mary's High School from 1926 to 1930, where he earned 11 varsity letters for several sports. He was offered college scholarships to play football and a pro contract to play for the Seattle Rainiers of the Pacific Coast League. Unfortunately, minor-league baseball did not pay well, and Valverde was forced to pass up professional baseball to support his family. He was inducted into both the Stockton Athletic Hall of Fame and the Stockton Mexican Sports Hall of Fame. (Courtesy of Louis A. Valverde.)

The 1956 team Club México played in the California Mexican Baseball League. The team members, seen here at Stribley Park in Stockton, are, from left to right, (first row) Mel Núñez, Ronnie Keil, Primo Orosco, batboy Louis Valverde, Ben Guerrero, Richard Valverde, and Matt Equinoa; (second row) José Zaragoza, Jim Reynosa Jr., Donnie Freed, Manuel Martín, Bob Lewright, Bill Stevens, Sahcus Orosco, and Ben Valverde. Several of these players were inducted into the Stockton Mexican Sports Hall of Fame, including Primo Orosco (2004), Matt Equinoa (2005), Ben Valverde (2006), Sachus Orosco (2007), and José Zaragoza (2008). (Courtesy of Louis A. Valverde.)

Albert Moreno from Tracy, California, was an outstanding player around the Central Valley of California. Yet, he loved to umpire, doing it for 53 years between 1961 and 2014. Moreno (first row, second from left) was inducted into the Oklahoma City Hall of Fame in 1989, the Stockton Wall of Honor in 1998, and the Tracy Sports Hall of Fame in 2014. The two other Mexican American umpires in this photograph are Frank Cortéz (first row, far left) and Rob Sánchez (first row, third from left.) (Courtesy of Albert Moreno.)

Sisters Margaret (third from left) and Eleanor Salazar (third from right) played ball in Pasadena, including the All-American Professional Softball League from 1944 to 1949. They are seen here in Phoenix, Arizona, in 1948. They attended Muir Technical School in Pasadena with Jackie Robinson. During World War II, Eleanor was a riveter, and Margaret worked in an office. Their father, David Salazar, pitched for the San Francisco Seals. Eleanor is the mother of Darrell Evans, who played in the major leagues for 20 years. (Courtesy of Carlos Salazar.)

Ray Armenta and his wife, Teresa de la Fuente, pose in 1933 before a game of the Tucson Tigers. It is believed that the team was comprised of former hometown residents living in Los Angeles. It was not unusual for teams to adopt the names of their former places of residence; this was especially true of towns in Mexico. Ray had two brothers on the team, Joe and Tony. Teresa, like many baseball wives, supported her husband with passion and attended the games with their children. Ray played for over 40 years. (Courtesy of Bea Armenta Dever.)

David Salazar (second row, third from right) played for this 1925 Arizona team in the Texas-Arizona Leagues. Salazar was born in 1895 near Griffith Park. His parents had come to Los Angeles from Jalisco, Mexico, in 1888. In the first part of the 20th century, the extended Salazar family produced an incredible number of extraordinary ballplayers, including Mike, Pete, and Ernie. David started playing in Mexico around 1920, working under the table for the Mexican government as a customs agent so he could play ball full-time. (Courtesy of Carlos Salazar.)

There were countless Mexican American teams in Colorado, Nebraska, Wyoming, and Montana, that played in several annual tournaments in the 1940s and 1950s. This 1948 Gilcrest Aztecs Juniors team played in the Pan-American Tournament. Shown here are, from left to right, (first row) Rudy Baldizan, Ray Sota, Richard Chacon, Benny Sota, and Maggie Domínguez; (second row) Hern Johns, Pete López, Joe Andrade, L. Álvarez, Glen Andrade, F. Chacon, B. Espinoza, and coach Phillip Martínez. (Courtesy of Gabriel and Jody López Collections.)

This 1952 photograph was taken at Island Grove Park. Among the players pictured are Joe Benavidez, Jerry Téllez, Robert Duran, Abe García, George Téllez, Leo Solís, David Madrid, Elías Espinosa Jr., Danny Téllez, Claudie García, Art Valdez, Sam López, Henry Martínez, Mickey Villa, Frank Carbajal, Robert Núañez, Leo Solís, Steve García, and Martín Hernández. Father Dominic from Our Lady of Peace used to get a bunch of kids together, like the Téllez brothers, some of the Garcías, and whoever wanted to play, and then travel to Eaton, Gilcrest, and La Salle to play other teams. (Courtesy of Gabriel and Jody López.)

The Ault Tigers in Colorado played for about 16 years. Their team manager was Ben Baca. They played their games at the Great Western sugar-beet dump, with homemade backstops made of chicken wire and wood posts. The bases were burlap bags filled with sawdust or dirt. The 1944 Tigers, shown here, are, from left to right, (first row) Salvador Martínez, Félix Martínez, Tony Baca, Fermín Baca, Paul Baca, and unidentified; (second row) Max Baca, unidentified, Manuel Martínez, Herman Baca, Charlie Díaz, and unidentified. (Courtesy of Gabriel and Jody López.)

The 1946 Greely Charros (Cowboys) are, from left to right, (first row) John Juárez, Ray Villa, Mike Esqubil, Dan Solíz, and Manuel Bajarano; (second row) coach Fred Olivas, Paul Sora, Julio Mendoza, Albert Muñoz, Ángel Alcarez, and Gunsi García. The batboy is Birdie Carbajal. (Courtesy of Gabriel, and Jody López.)

The 1943 Cheyenne (Wyoming) Lobos (Wolves) played their games on vacant lots and at Pioneer Park. They played several teams from both Colorado and Nebraska. Posing for a team photograph are, from left to right, (first row) Louie Montoya and Roy Salazar; (second row) Paul García, George Armijo, Joe Borego, Danny Padilla, Joe Salazar, unidentified, and manager Joe Bustos; (third row) scorekeeper Louie Rodríguez, Philip Mercado, Tony Sánchez, Benny Salazar, Julio Abeyta, Joe Ramírez, and unidentified. (Courtesy of Gabriel and Jody López.)

The 1945 Milliken Caballeros (Gentlemen) were one of the original teams of the Pan American Baseball League, which comprised squads from Northern Colorado. Admission was free, and people parked their automobiles around the perimeter of the field. Picnics were held at the games. Shown here are, from left to right, (first row) Benny Fresquez, Raymond Belo, Juan Fresquez, Joe Serreno, and Ralph Solano; (second row), two unidentified, Victor Serrano, and Mario ?; (third row) unidentified, Johnny Lovato, Adolph Belo, and Gilder Serreno. (Courtesy of Gabriel and Jody López.)

The Gilcrest Aztecs date to the 1920s. Between Eaton and Brighton, Colorado, the Great Western Company had four major factories harvesting sugar beets. Baseball was one of the cheapest forms of entertainment. The players would work 20 extra acres of beets in order to buy baseball equipment. They played throughout Colorado and Wyoming. The 1933 Aztecs are, from left to right, (first row) Rufus Peñaflor, Lino Peñaflor, John López, Mike Soto, and Alfred García; (second row) Jack Chacon, Dave Peñaflor, Tony Andrade, Tony Federico, Ray Chacon, Manuel Hernández, Tony López, and Marcelino Romero. (Courtesy of Gabriel and Jody López.)

The 1952 Greeley Grays of Colorado once played a game in Wheatland, Wyoming, where they were called "beet pickers" and other derogatory names. The Grays responded by beating the team so badly, the Grays had to be escorted out of town. They played their games at Gipson Park. Pictured are, from left to right, (first row) Ray Talmadge, Arnulfo López, Bob Fetch, Augustine López, Ricardo Rico, and Louis Espinosa; (second row) David López, Tito García, Frank López, Silvestre Gramaldo, Jimmy Mock, Robert Lind, George Villa, Jess González, and John Lohr. (Courtesy of Gabriel and Jody López.)

The 1946 Fort Collins Legionnaires were an outstanding team in Colorado. Mexican American teams date back to the 1930s, with the Fort Collins Spanish American Club. Pictured are, from left to right, (first row) Lee Zúñiga, Sal Blanco, Tony Baca, Lloyd Jirón, Luís Martínez, Jess Peña, and Nick Peña; (second row) Max Baca, Frank Blanco, Augie Blanco, Richard Maxwell, Bob Roybal, Rudy Martínez, and manager Lambert Álvarez. (Courtesy of Gabriel and Jody López.)

The Longmont Merchants were a freelance team playing hardball at Roosevelt Field at the fairgrounds. Nearly all of the players had worked in the beet fields. They played in the Rocky Mountain League, which was affiliated with the National Baseball Congress in Wichita, Kansas. Their opponents included the Greeley Grays, Wattonburg Bluejays, Gill Indians, Gilcrest Aztecs, Milliken Caballeros, Kersey Primos, Ault Tigers, Fort Collins Legionnaires, Cheyenne Lobos, and Greeley Charros. (Courtesy of Gabriel and Jody López.)

The Mexican Catholics, a Newton, Kansas, team, are seen here in 1947 playing at Athletic Park. Standing at right is Maggie Gómez. On the bench are, from left to right, Frank Rodríguez, Manuel Pérez, Lidio Jaso, and Lalo Viramontes. Many of these players worked at the Atchison, Topeka & Santa Fe Railroad, located across the street from the ballpark. They worked at the rail mill making rails for the trains. Athletic Park is home to the oldest continuous Mexican American fast-pitch tournament in the United States. (Courtesy of Rod Martínez.)

This St. Mary's team from Newton, Kansas, won the parochial championship in Bentley, Kansas. Among those pictured are Julián Arellano, Nick Sauceda, Pete Estrada, Rubén Carrión, Father Abraham, head coach Billie S. Lujano, Raymond Arellano, Louis Sandoval Sr., and Ralph Pérez. Julián Arellano was one of the best Mexican American athletes, helping his team win the Kansas State high school football championship in 1955. (Courtesy of Ali Solís.)

The 1935 Kansas City, Missouri, West Side youth team was sponsored by the Guadalupe Parochial School. The school competed in the Kansas City Catholic Parochial League. The Guadalupe Centers Inc., founded in the 1920s, is the oldest continuously operated Mexican American community service agency on the west side. Only a handful of these players have been identified: Vince Guerra (first row, far left), Erie López (first row, second from left), Ralph Hernandez (second row, far left), "Cuco" Hernández (second row, fourth from left), and the coach, Mr. Berkman (second row, far right.) (Courtesy of Guadalupe Centers Inc.)

Members of the 1955 Kansas City team leave for a road trip to Omaha, Nebraska. Players came from both Kansas and Missouri and felt a connection, especially after a flood in the Kaw Valley forced many residents from Kansas to resettle on the Missouri side. Shown here are, from left to right, (first row) Chuck Lombrano, Joe Campos, Manuel Mejia, ? Montéz, and Silvester Ayala; (second row) Nick Ramírez, Manual Zúñiga, Jesse Salas, Tony Cecena Jr., Mickey Cisneros, Joe Morales, Richard Cecena, and unidentified. (Courtesy of Gene Chávez.)

The Stateline Locos were organized in an area of Kansas City, Kansas, called the West Bottoms. It was part of the greater Mexican American community of Argentine, Armourdale, Rosedale, and Kansas City, Missouri's, West Side. Members of the 1948 Locos are, from left to right, (first row) Robert Lombrano, Tony López, John Duran, Fred Lombrano, Pete Rodríguez, and "Lefty" Montes; (second row) Nieves Valdez, Richard Ríos, David Segura, Chuck Lombrano, Tony Segura, unidentified, Carlos Montes, and Félix Ortega. (Courtesy of R. Ramírez.)

The Yaquis, the Mayas, the Excelsiors, and the Atlas in the 1930s were as familiar to the Mexican American community in South Chicago as the Cubs, Sox, Bears, and Bulls are today. Mexican Eustebio Torres and Eduardo Peralta organized men's athletic teams and leagues. At least one all-girl league existed. (Courtesy of the Southeast Chicago Project and Michael D. Innis-Jiménez.)

Members of a men's baseball team wear uniforms featuring the names of Our Lady of Guadalupe and St. Jude in the late 1940s. The two names are used somewhat interchangeably, but St. Jude refers to the National Shrine of St. Jude, established by Father Torte. Sports were supported by both the Chicago Park District and by other churches in the diocese.

7

FIELD OF DREAMS

The roots of the Latino Baseball History Project can be traced to an event that took place at California State University–Los Angeles in 2006. A three-month exhibit entitled "Mexican American Baseball in East Los Angeles" had been sponsored by both the Chicano Studies department and the Baseball Reliquary. As a result of this successful exhibit, a core of community and university historians and scholars established the Mexican American Baseball History Project. Because of funding considerations, the project changed its name to the Latino Baseball History Project. Nevertheless, the project centers exclusively on Mexican American baseball and softball.

The project was initially housed at California State University–Los Angeles. For the last five years, it has been on the campus of California State University–San Bernardino.

The Latino Baseball History Project is involved with several activities to promote the long and rich history of Mexican American ball, including public exhibits, newsletters, books, conferences, oral interviews, college courses, and photograph collections. To date, the project has collected over 3,000 photographs dating to the 1870s. From the beginning, the mission of the project has been to explore the social, cultural, gender, and political roles of baseball and softball from the 19th century through the 1950s, a period of racial segregation and intense struggle for civil and labor rights.

Through its book series, the project has attracted outstanding community and university scholars to write exceptional chapters on specific communities, as well as on themes including military, women, college, the border, professionals, and labor. At first, the project concentrated its research efforts on California; nevertheless, each of the first five California books included a chapter, "Coast to Coast," that highlighted baseball and softball in several states outside of California prior to the 1960s. The project is now working with baseball and softball researchers in Texas for a series of books, including this first one.

The project is currently collaborating with scholars in Kansas, Colorado, Nebraska, Illinois, and Indiana. Each of the project's books concludes with a chapter that shows the players and families as they are today. We honor and pay tribute to all of these extraordinary players and their families, wherever they are.

The Quad Cities, on the Iowa-Illinois border, have produced outstanding players and teams. Mexican Americans settled in Bettendorf and Davenport, Iowa, and in Silvis and Moline, Illinois, working on the railroads, in manufacturing, and in agriculture. These communities sent men to World War II, Korea, and Vietnam. Silvis is the home of the famous Hero Street, named for the large number of Mexican Americans who have served in the military. Some of these former players and/or veterans are, from left to right, Tanilo Sandoval, Michael Cervantes, and Joe and Bennie Terronez. (Courtesy of Michael Cervantes.)

Jesse Gallardo (right) played and coached for the city of Soledad, California, for over 50 years. He competed against other Mexican American teams from the Central Coast and the Central Valley. He coached youth ball and local school teams. Because of his unselfish commitment to the community, a park was named in his honor. Fred Ledesma (left), the mayor of Soledad, played with and against Jesse. Ledesma was a baseball star at Gonzáles High School and at Hartnell Junior College in 1977–1978. (Courtesy of Richard A. Santillán.)

The Mexican American community in Claremont, California, sponsored an event in 2012 to honor former players. Here, California state senator Gloria Negrete-McCloud presents a plaque from the state legislature to Dr. Richard A. Santillán, recognizing the amazing contributions of the players shown here. They are, from left to right, Richard García, Tommie Encinas, Maury Encinas, Steven Villanueva, Rudy Gómez, Ignacio Félix, John Hernández, Gil Candelas, Gilbert Guevara, and Chuck Briones. (Courtesy of Susan Brunasso.)

The San Gabriel Historical Association held an event in 2014 at the Mission, paying tribute to outstanding players. From left to right are (first row) unidentified, Lucy Pedregón, Irene Aguirre Juárez, Margarte Barrera Sosa, Dolí Juárez Acuna, Virginia Acuna Flores, and Camila Alva López; (second row) Enrique López, Bob Lagunas, Rod Martínez, Al Padilla, Carlos Salazar, and Tom Pérez Jr. Irene is the sister of Hank Aguirre, Margaret is the daughter of Joe Barrera, Virginia is the daughter of Big Joe Acuna, and Camilia is the granddaughter of Mike Salazar. (Courtesy of Rod Martínez.)

In 2014, the Mexican American community of Santa Maria sponsored an exhibit, a forum, and a book-signing event at the Santa Maria Library. Players and families came from all over the Santa Maria Valley. Gathered here are, from left to right, (first row) Vincent Galván, Gerald Rodrigues, Ernie Baldievez, Eddie Navarro, Rudy Galván, Art Manríguez, Blas Torres, James Bartlett, and Jim Zedpeda; (second row) Ariston Julián, Dorothy Romero, Betty Estés Silva, Art Amarillas, Paul Béndele, Al Ramos, Rennie Pili, Richard Noriega, Joe Béndele, and John Lizalde. (Courtesy of Maria Navarro.)

In the summer of 2014, an exhibit and book-signing event was held at the Guadalupe Cultural Center. Players and families came from throughout the Santa Maria Valley. In this photograph are, from left to right, Art Manríguez, Rudy Martínez, Delbert Corella, Mickey Pardo, Greg Orosco, Rudy Galván, Moses Hidalgo, Al Ramos, Joe Talaugon, James Bartlett, Ron Escobedo, Blas Torres, Ernie Corral, Sylvester Orosco, Tony Villegas Sr. and Jr., Tommy Martínez, Eddie Navarro, Art Delgadillo, John Álvarado, John Lizalde, Art Amarillas, Richard A. Santillán, and Rennie Pili. (Courtesy of Maria Navarro.)

In 2014, a book signing and panel discussion were sponsored by the Mexican American Sports Hall of Fame in Sacramento, California. Several players spoke about how baseball and softball had affected their personal, family, and community lives. All of the participants said that baseball had a positive outcome in their careers and that the lessons they learned on the field applied to life outside the diamond. On the panel are, from left to right, Ernie Cervantes, Rachel Cervantes-Wallin, Cuno Barragán, and Eric and Eddie Cervantes. (Courtesy of Richard A. Santillán.)

The city of Corona, California, has a long and rich history of Mexican American baseball and softball. The Corona Historical Society, along with several community groups, has sponsored events showcasing this wonderful history, including this 2013 meeting. Gathered here are, from left to right, (first row) Chayo Rodríguez, Genovieve Brock, and unidentified; (second row) Remi Álvarez, Carlos Uribe, Richard Cortéz, Rey León, and Richard A. Santillán. Brock is the widow of one of Chayo's former players, Nick Serrato, who graduated from Corona High School in 1972. (Courtesy of Don Williamson.)

In 2013, a planning meeting was held at the San Fernando Museum of Art and History for a future baseball book on both the city of San Fernando and the greater San Fernando Valley. Several people brought their photographs and stories to share with the Latino Baseball History Project. Shown here are, from left to right, (seated) Joffee García, Mary Jo Moss, and Kim Paine; (standing) Richard Arroyo, Chris Docter, Terry Bacon, Alice Cruz Bacon, Vickie Carrillo Norton, Joe Govea, and Veto Ruiz. (Courtesy of Richard A. Santillán.)

In 2014, a book-signing event was held at the San Fernando Museum of Art and History for the book *Mexican American Baseball in the Central Coast*, which included a chapter on the San Fernando Valley. Posing here are, from left to right, (first row) Richard Arroyo, Benny Salas, Flora Talamantes, Joffee García, Alice Cruz Bacon, Vickie Carrillo Norton, David González, Rudy Aragón, and Rubén Ruiz; (second row) Chris Docter, Louie Cervantes, Ángela Cervantes, Rod Martínez, Yolanda García, Ramona Cervantes, Veto Ruiz, Marty Cortinas, Julie Alba González, unidentified, Mark Barraza Jr., Pete Prieto, and Andy Alba. (Courtesy of Richard A. Santillán.)

In October 2014, a book signing was held at the home of Ramona Cervantes in Arleta, California. Gathered here for a photograph are, from left to right, (first row) Stella Quijada, Alex Sáenz, Minnie Moreno, and Terry Hernández; (second row) Marty Cortines, Yolanda García, Rosie Rico, Ramona Valenzuela Cervantes, Michael Ramírez, Moe Murietta, Joffee García, Louie Cervantes, and Ángela Cervantes. Residents in San Fernando Valley communities are currently collecting photographs and stories for a future book on Mexican American baseball and softball. This research effort is headed by Christopher Docter, Vickie Carrillo Norton, and Richard Arroyo. (Courtesy of Richard A. Santillán.)

Phyllis Pérez comes from a family of ballplayers who competed in Colorado, Nebraska, Montana, and Wyoming in the 1930s through the 1950s. Like so many others, she has been a good friend of the Latino Baseball History Project, sponsoring several book-signing events over the past four years in the Modesto and Riverbank communities. In this 2011 photograph are, from left to right, Dr. Richard A. Santillán, Rosie Munguía, Gary Sandoval, Olivia Sandoval, Lupe Pérez, Phyllis Pérez, Nadien Ulloa, Eddie Ulloa, and Junior Ulloa. (Courtesy of Richard A. Santillán.)

In 2011, Cal Poly Pomona sponsored its first baseball exhibit and community luncheon to honor six players with extraordinary experiences and credentials. Each has devoted his entire life to promoting baseball and softball to the youth of the community. Standing here are, from left to right, Tommie Encinas from Pomona, Ignacio Félix from Claremont, Richard Peña from East Los Angeles, Bob Lagunas from Pico Rivera, Al Padilla from East Los Angeles, and Maury Encinas from Pomona. In the background is the exhibit highlighting their amazing careers. (Courtesy of Manny Veron.)

In 2011, a ceremony was held at Belvedere Park in East Los Angeles honoring Manuel "Shorty" Pérez, longtime baseball manager and former player. A memorial plaque highlighting his 35-year career (1947–1981) was unveiled by Los Angeles County supervisor Gloria Molina (seated at left), along with other dignitaries. Richard A. Santillán (left) and Francisco E. Balderrama are at the podium. Terry A. Cannon (second from right), executive director of the Baseball Reliquary, helped spearhead the memorial, along with Shorty's son, Gilbert (far right). (Courtesy of Latino Baseball History Project.)

FIELD OF DREAMS

Since 2011, California State University–Pomona has sponsored an annual event paying tribute to men and women who have contributed to the rich and long history of Mexican American baseball and softball. These events are sponsored by both the ethnic and women's studies department, and the Cesar E. Chávez Center. The 2014 event was entitled "The Boys and Girls of Summer: Mexican American Baseball and Softball in the Pomona Valley, 1930s–1970s." Shown here are several of the players and family representatives who attended. (Courtesy of Manny Veron.)

For the past three years, California State University–Pomona has offered a class on the history of Mexican American baseball and softball and their impact on civil and political rights. In 2014, three outstanding players were invited to speak to the class. Sandra Uribe served as moderator, due to her excellent research on women and softball. Teresa Santillán has been a longtime member of the Latino Baseball History Project. From left to right are Sandra Uribe, Patti Encinas García, Estela Elías Acosta, Margaret Villa Cryan, and Teresa Santillán. (Courtesy of Estela Elías Acosta.)

In 2014, the city of Pomona, California, hosted a book signing celebrating the release of *Mexican American Baseball in the Pomona Valley*. Several outstanding former players from the Pomona Valley attended and shared their wonderful stories. Gathered here are, from left to right, Richard García, Patti Encinas García, Estela Elías Acosta, Gilbert Guevara, Buddy Muñoz, Alejo L. Vásquez, Joey Fuentes, Alfonso Guevara, and Mike Guevara. (Courtesy of Estela Elías Acosta.)

In 2014, the Montebello Historical Society recognized several outstanding players and their families. Some of them shared wonderful and funny stories of former playing days. Seen here are, from left to right, (first row) Consuelo Solís, Ray Ramírez, David Contreras, Fidel Elizarrez, and Al Padilla; (second row) Bob Lagunas, James David Aguirre, Charlie Sierra, unidentified, Davey Escobedo, Joséph Holguín, and Armando Pérez. (Courtesy of Richard A. Santillán.)

These are four of the original Orange Tomboys team of 1947. They are, from left to right, Carolina García, Emma Félix, unidentified, and Lucy Duran. Duran graduated from Orange Union High School in 1947 and played for the school's baseball, volleyball, soccer, and basketball teams. She has seen five of her grandchildren play baseball and softball. García graduated in 1949. Félix still lives in Orange. On the Tomboys, Duran played shortstop, Félix was in center field, and García played third base. Duran's and Félix's cousin Lupe pitched, and their sister Delia played outfield. (Courtesy of Richard A. Santillán.)

Ramona Cervantes has been a longtime supporter of the Latino Baseball Project, hosting book-signing events at her home. These gatherings have brought together many former players from the San Fernando Valley. At one such event in 2012, two women brought their 1940s uniforms to share with the crowd. Seen here are, from left to right, Flora Hernández Talamantes from the North Hollywood Huskies, Nellie García and Isabel Vaíz Mejía from the San Fernando Blue Jays, Teresa Hernández Ruiz from Barrio Orcasitas, and Ramona Valenzuela Cervantes from the North Hollywood Vixies. (Courtesy of Richard A. Santillán.)

In 2013, a symposium was held at Lincoln Park in East Los Angeles entitled "Neighborhoods of Baseball," exploring the inter-ethnic relationship of baseball among African Americans, Asian Americans, and Mexican Americans. Dr. Samuel O. Regalado, professor of history, gave the keynote address. There were three panels examining the various roles that ball played in the lives of these three distinct communities. On this panel are, from left to right, moderator Dr. Jorge Iber, Daryl Grigsby, Kerry Yo Nakagawa, Bill Staples Jr., Sandra Uribe, and Dr. Richard A. Santillán. (Courtesy of Jesse Saucedo.)

In 2005, a dinner was held to honor the original Greeley Grays Colorado teams from 1938–1969. At the top of the stairs are members of the 2005 team. The others are, from left to right, (first row) Dr. Jim Lochner, Tito García Jr., Frank López, Scruffy the Grays Squirrel, Palmer López, and Silvestri Gramaldo; (second row) Bill Crosier, Richard López, Sam López, Dr. Gil Carbajal, Robert Nuañez, and Arnulfo López; (third row) Frank Carbajal, Claudie García, Abe García, Alvin García, Jack Steele, and Dwight Steele. Behind them are Gene Swanson and Cornell Sullivan. (Courtesy of Gabriel and Jody López Collections.)

A game was held at the University High School baseball field to honor several members of the Greeley Grays. Posing here are, from left to right, Ed Dyer, John Barnes, Gene Swanson, Tito García Jr., Bill Crosier, Palmer López, Tony Chacon, Dwight Steele, Abe García, Richard López, Arnulfo López, Robert Nuañez, Matt Mares, and Don Foster. The honoring of the original Grays started in 2006. This year will mark the 10th anniversary of paying tribute to these remarkable players. (Courtesy of Gabriel and Jody López Collections.)

In 2013, the Gabe and Jody Sugar Beet League exhibit was held in Brighton, Colorado. Shaking hands are, from left to right, Greeley Grays Richard López, Arnulfo López (Fort Lupton Eagles), Tony Ortega, and Junior Márquez. Gabe and Jody López have sponsored exhibits at the Greeley Museums, the Cheyenne Civic Center, the University of Wyoming Chicano Studies department, the Cheyenne Train Depot Museum, and the University of Northern Colorado Library. In 2013, Gabe and Jody López spoke at the National Baseball Hall of Fame in Cooperstown, New York. (Courtesy of Gabriel and Jody López Collections.)

ABOUT THE ORGANIZATION

Members of the History Project Advisory Board are as follows: José M. Alamillo, associate professor, California State University–Channel Islands; Gabriel "Tito" Ávila Jr., founding president and CEO, Hispanic Heritage Baseball Museum, San Francisco; Francisco E. Balderrama, professor, California State University–Los Angeles; Tomas Benítez, artist and art consultant; Anna Bermúdez, curator, Museum of Ventura County; Terry A. Cannon, executive director of the Baseball Reliquary; Gene Aguilera, Mexican American boxing historian; Raúl J. Córdova, dean, Los Angeles Trade-Technical College; Christopher Docter, graduate student in history, California State University–Northridge; Prof. Peter Drier, Occidental College; Prof. Robert Elias, University of San Francisco; Luís F. Fernández, public historian; Jorge Iber, associate dean and professor, Texas Tech University; Alfonso Ledesma, Cucamonga public historian; Enrique M. López, University of California–Riverside; Jody L. and Gabriel A. López, Mexican American sugar-beet labor/baseball historians, Rocky Mountain States; Susan C. Luévano, librarian, California State University–Long Beach; Amanda Magdalena, doctorate student in history, University of Buffalo, the State University of New York; Douglas Monroy, Colorado College; Carlos Muñoz Jr., professor emeritus, University of California–Berkeley; Eddie Navarro, sports historian, Santa Maria; Mark A. Ocegueda, doctorate student in history, University of California–Irvine; Alan O'Connor, sports historian, Sacramento; Mónica Ortez, Orange County public historian; Al Ramos, Santa Maria Valley historian; Prof. Samuel O. Regalado, California State University–Stanislaus; Vicki L. Ruiz, distinguished professor of history and Chicano and Latino studies, University of California–Irvine; Anthony Salazar, Latino Baseball Committee, Society of American Baseball Research; Richard A. Santillán, professor emeritus, California State University–Pomona; Marcelino Saucedo, Catalina Island historian; Joe Talaugon, Guadalupe Cultural Arts and Educational Center/Sports Hall of Fame; Carlos Tortolero, president, Mexican Fine Arts Center Museum, Chicago; Prof. Sandra L. Uribe, Westwood College, South Bay Campus, Torrance, California; Alejo L. Vásquez, Cucamonga public historian; Prof. Angelina F. Veyna, Santa Ana College; and Alfonso Villanueva Jr., Árbol Verde Committee, Claremont.

BIBLIOGRAPHY

Aguilera, Gene. *Mexican American Boxing in Los Angeles*. Charleston, SC: Arcadia Publishing, 2014.

Byerly, Ed. "Three Nines and a Diamond: The Ways, Means, and Consequences of Segregated Baseball in Victoria, Texas." *Journal of South Texas*.

El Bronco Yearbook Collection, 1928–1971. Edinburg, TX: Pan American University. Published annually. Lower Rio Grande Valley Collection, the University of Texas–Pan American.

El Paladin. Community newspaper, Corpus Christi, TX: 1929.

El Sentinel. Community newspaper, Corpus Christi, TX: 1948.

Iber, Jorge, Samuel O. Regalado, José M. Alamillo, and Arnoldo De Leon. *Latinos in U.S. Sport: A History of Isolation, Cultural Identity, and Acceptance*. Champaign, IL: Human Kinetics, 2011.

Longoria, Mario. *Athletes Remembered: Mexicano/Latino Professional Football Players, 1929–1970*. Tempe, AZ: Bilingual Press, 1997.

López, Jody L. and Gabriel A. *From Sugar to Diamonds: Spanish/Mexican Baseball 1925–1969*. Bloomington, IN: AuthorHouse, 2009.

Martínez-García, Christy. "On an Equal Playing Field: Las Estrellas–The Stars, Lubbock's First All-Latina Baseball Team." *Latino Lubbock*, March 2009.

O'Neil, Dick "Lefty." *Dreaming of the Majors, Living in the Bush: A Life's Journey Through the Negro Leagues with His Guardian Angels*. WinePress Publishing, 2009.

Rio Grande Valley Sports Hall of Fame: 2014.

Santillán, Richard, et al. *Mexican American Baseball in the Pomona Valley*. Charleston, SC: Arcadia Publishing, 2014.

Taylor, Paul Schuster. *An American Mexican Frontier*. Nueces, Texas.

Taylor, Rick. "The '49 Bowie Bears: City's Only State Baseball Champions." *El Paso Times*. June 10, 1992.

The Brownsville Herald. Editorial, 2000–2014.

The Cactus Yearbook Collection: 1901–1980. Austin: TX: Dabney. Published annually. Briscoe Center for American History.

Torres, Rene. Personal collection. Brownsville, TX: 2014.

Visit us at
arcadiapublishing.com

www.ingramcontent.com/pod-product-compliance
Lightning Source LLC
Chambersburg PA
CBHW050655110426
42813CB00007B/2022